LYNCHBURG COLLEGE LIBRARY
WITHDRAWN

TWAYNE'S WORLD AUTHORS SERIES

A Survey of the World's Literature

Sylvia E. Bowman, Indiana University

GENERAL EDITOR

NEW ZEALAND

Joseph Jones, University of Texas at Austin

EDITOR

James K. Baxter

TWAS 384

Sketch by Els Noordhof

James Baxter

JAMES K. BAXTER

By CHARLES DOYLE
Victoria University

TWAYNE PUBLISHERS
A DIVISION OF G. K. HALL & CO., BOSTON

Copyright © 1976 by G. K. Hall & Co.
All Rights Reserved
First Printing

Library of Congress Cataloging in Publication Data

Doyle, Charles, 1928 -
  James K. Baxter.

  (Twayne's world authors series ; TWAS 384 : New Zealand)
  Bibliography: p. 179 - 83.
  Includes index.
  1. Baxter, James K. — Criticism and interpretation. I. Title.
PR9639.3.B3Z63   821   75-33781
ISBN 0-8057-6227-2

Dedicated to Louis Johnson

Contents

About the Author
Preface
Acknowledgments
Chronology
Abbreviations
1 Life 19
2 The Early Poetry 37
3 The Door Ajar to Let the Furies Enter 55
4 That Wild Interior Island 72
5 In Quest of the Just City 88
6 A Cell of Good Living 100
7 The Virgin and the Witch 118
8 Unveiling Chaos: Baxter's Drama 134
9 The Way to the Upper Room 149
Notes and References 171
Glossary of Maori Words 177
Appendix 178
Selected Bibliography 179
Index 185

About the Author

A New Zealander by adoption, Charles Doyle has a Ph.D. from Auckland University. A poet in his own right, he collaborated with James K. Baxter and Louis Johnson in editing the literary periodical *Numbers* (1954-1959). In 1958-59 Doyle travelled in the U.S.A. on a UNESCO Artist's Fellowship and in 1967-68 he was an American Council of Learned Societies Fellow and Visiting Fellow in American Studies at Yale University. At present he is an Associate Professor of English at the University of Victoria, British Columbia, Canada. While working on this book he returned to New Zealand for part of the 1974-75 academic year, with the aid of a Canada Council Leave Fellowship.

Doyle's publications include a number of volumes of poetry, an anthology of *Recent Poetry in New Zealand* (1965), *R.A.K. Mason* (Twayne's World Authors Series, 1970), *William Carlos Williams: The Critical Heritage* (forthcoming from Routledge & Kegan Paul, London), and articles and reviews in *Renascence, Modern Poetry Studies, Perspective, ARIEL: A Review of International English Literature, Poetry* (Chicago), *Canadian Literature* and *American Quarterly*. From 1969 to 1974 he edited the poetry magazine *Tuatara*. He is at present revising a study of Williams's poetics.

Preface

Widely considered to be New Zealand's foremost poet, James K. Baxter is also one of the most remarkable English-language poets of the mid-twentieth century. Still an accolade for a New Zealand writer, four selections of his poetry were published in London by Oxford University Press. More important perhaps, he became an esteemed and loved figure in his own country both for his writings and his commitment to action as a Christian humanist. Baxter was my contemporary and when he died in 1972 he was only 46 years old; but his publications cover a thirty-year span and his quite long literary career bore fruit in many volumes of poems, a good number of plays, four separate works of literary commentary or criticism, quite a large number of essays on religious topics, and a small amount of fiction. The present book is the first full-length study of Baxter's writings, and one that was begun with his blessing. My central intention is to offer a coherent introduction to his published work as a whole, and to illuminate that work where I can. I have been fortunate in having access to the Baxter Papers in the Hocken Library, University of Otago, though there is an understandable restriction on extensive quotation from the writings so far unpublished.

Baxter is both an engaging writer and an important one. His life and work merit, and will afford, further study. A few years ago J. E. Weir published a useful small monograph on *The Poetry of James K. Baxter*. If the present study serves just as usefully as an introduction to the whole corpus of Baxter's published writing, I shall have achieved my aim.

Acknowledgments

To Mrs. Jacquie Baxter and the estate of the late James K. Baxter for permission to quote from published works and to have access to unpublished materials, and to Mrs. Baxter for consultation in matters of detail; to Mr. Patric Carey of the Globe Theatre, Dunedin, for the loan of materials and for consultation; to Mr. Michael Hitchings, Librarian, and the Hocken Library, University of Otago, for access to the Baxter Papers and for other services; to Lisa and Denis Rose for provision of materials and for friendly assistance; for materials to Professor Philip Smithells, University of Otago, Professor Bert Almon, University of Alberta, and Mr. John Summers of Christchurch, New Zealand; to Mr. Kendrick Smithyman, University of Auckland and Father F. M. McKay, Victoria University of Wellington; to my wife, Doran Ross Doyle, for reading and commenting on the text.

I would like to thank also the Canada Council for a Leave Fellowship, part of which was used to work on this book; the University of Victoria, B.C., for sabbatical leave and research funds, both of which helped toward the writing of the book; the University of Auckland, which provided Library and Common Room facilities during a five-month stay; the University of Canterbury, which made available a copy of J. E. Weir's thesis on Baxter.

Finally, I wish to pay tribute to the late James K. Baxter, who agreed in 1970 to my working on this book, and with whom I enjoyed a measure of friendship and a long period of association, for some years in day-to-day contact as writers and, latterly, by correspondence. As this is a paragraph of tribute I mention again my wife, for whose personal support during the past two years I shall always be grateful.

As always, of course, a writer's shortcomings in any book he may produce are entirely his own.

Chronology

1926	James Keir Baxter born 29 June 1926 at Brighton, Otago.
1933 - 1937	Attended school at Brighton. At seven discovered vocation as poet. Later sent to board at St John's, a Quaker school, in Wanganui.
1937 - 1939	Baxter family lived in England. James Baxter attended a Quaker school in the Cotswolds.
1939	Gollancz published Archibald Baxter's autobiography, *We Will Not Cease*, in London. The Baxter family returned to New Zealand.
1940	Baxter attended St John's School, Wanganui, for a further year.
1941 - 1943	Student at King's High School, Dunedin.
1944	Enrolled at Otago University. Awarded MacMillan Brown Prize for "Convoys." Poems in *Critic* and *Otago University Review*. Baxter's *Night Shift* poems apparently written at this period. *Beyond the Palisade* published. Contact with Ormond Burton and A. R. D. Fairburn.
1945	Worked in the rolling mill at Green Island, Dunedin. Six poems included in Allen Curnow's *A Book of New Zealand Verse*. Poems in *Arts Yarbook* and *The Arts in New Zealand*.
1946	"Song for Otago University" published in *Book* and set to music by Douglas Lilburn. Met Charles Brasch.
1947	First publication in the new *Landfall: A New Zealand Quarterly*.
1948	Worked briefly at Christchurch *Press*, then very briefly as brass tap grinder. Unemployed, subsisted for a time on bottles of milk. Student at Canterbury University College. Poems and prose in *Canta, Canterbury University College Review*, and elsewhere. *Blow, Wind of Fruitfulness* pub-

	lished. Married Jacqueline Sturm, whom he had met in Dunedin. Met Denis Glover, Allen Curnow, Colin McCahon.
1949	Moved to Wellington (late 1948). Birth of his daughter, Hilary. Poems, stories, and reviews in *Hilltop, New Zealand Listener, Landfall,* and elsewhere. Met Louis Johnson, Alistair Campbell, and other members of the "Wellington group." Worked as a freezing-worker.
1950	Now published widely in periodicals. Worked as a postman. Began association with Anton Vogt, poet, English lecturer, and founder of Glenco Press.
1951	Student at Victoria University College, where he met Fleur Adcock, and the present writer. Anthologized in the Australasian *Jindyworobak Anthology* and in enlarged edition of Curnow's. Participated in Christchurch Writers' Conference. Published *Recent Trends in New Zealand Poetry.* Met George Hughes.
1952	Continued as student. Birth of son, John. Published *Poems Unpleasant* with Louis Johnson and Anton Vogt. Contributed to Johnson's *New Zealand Poetry Yearbook.*
1953	Teaching. Continued as student. *The Fallen House* published. Poems in *Meanjin Papers* (Australia).
1954	Helped initiate the periodical *Numbers,* coedited with Louis Johnson and Charles Doyle. Broadsheet "Lament for Barney Flanagan."
1955	Published *The Fire and the Anvil* (MacMillan Brown Lectures). Published *Traveller's Litany.* Work at School Publications.
1956	First publication of "Jack Winter's Dream," *Landfall,* September. That year published four short stories. Represented in Chapman and Bennett's *Oxford Book of New Zealand Verse.*
1957	Published *The Night Shift* with Charles Doyle, Louis Johnson, and Kendrick Smithyman. Published *The Iron Breadboard.* Six copies of a long-playing recording of Baxter reading made at Pilgrim Press, Auckland, by Brian Bell.
1958	Stay at Trappist monastery at Kopua, Hawke's Bay. Conversion to Roman Catholicism. Broadcast of "Jack Winter's Dream." UNESCO travel to India and Japan. *In Fires of No Return* published in London. *Chosen Poems* published in Bombay.

Chronology

1959   *Two Plays* published. "Aspects of Indian Life," in *Education*, June. Peter Bland and Erik Schwimmer joined editorial committee of *Numbers*. *Numbers* attacked for publishing stories of "illicit love." Voluntarily refused renewal of Literary Fund grant. Ceased publication.

1960   Represented in the *Penguin Book of New Zealand Verse*. A second essay on India published in *Education*.

1961   Broadcast of play, "The Silver Plate." *Howrah Bridge and Other Poems* published.

1962   Left School Publications to work as postman and mail sorter. New York production of *The Wide Open Cage*.

1963   Auckland English Association Poetry School with A. D. Hope and Ronald Tamplin. Death of Bob Lowry. Member of State Literary Fund Committee. Resigned due to controversy over grant to *Poetry Yearbook* (three of five poems objected to were his own). Later withdrew resignation.

1964   *Poems* published. Rimbaud translations published in *Landfall*. Poems in *London Magazine*.

1965   Autobiographical "Beginnings" in September *Landfall*. Represented in *Recent Poetry in New Zealand*. Poems in *London Magazine*. Series of religious articles in *Marist Messenger*. Many published poems, reviews, etc.

1966   Returned to Dunedin to take up Burns Fellowship. *Pig Island Letters* published. "Recollections of School Days" published in *Monthly Review*. Poems in *Poetry Australia* and elsewhere, also prose and reviews.

1967   New York and Wellington productions of *The Spots on the Leopard*. Globe Theatre, Dunedin, produced Baxter's mimes, and *The Band Rotunda, The Sore-Footed Man, The Bureaucrat, The Devil and Mr Mulcahy*, and presented "An Evening with Baxter." Continued Burns Fellowship for second year. Published *The Man on the Horse, The Lion Skin*, and *Aspects of New Zealand Poetry*.

1968   Globe Theatre put on a Baxter Festival of three plays and two mimes. Remained in Dunedin doing catechetical work.

1969   Baxter's "identity crisis" (*Dominion*). *The Rock Woman* published. *The Flowering Cross* published.

1970   To Jerusalem. Globe production of *The Temptations of Oedipus*. Represented in the *Oxford Book of New Zealand Verse*. Published *Jerusalem Sonnets*.

1971   Four plays published by Heinemann in two volumes. *Jeru-*

	salem Daybook published. Jerusalem activities curtailed and Baxter left for Wellington.
1972	At Jerusalem with smaller group. Published *Six Faces of Love, Ode to Auckland and Other Poems, Letter to Peter Olds, Autumn Testament.* James K. Baxter (Hemi) died 22 October 1972 at Grafton, Auckland. Funeral and burial at Jerusalem attended by hundreds from all over New Zealand. Memorial services in Auckland and Wellington.
1973	*Two Obscene Poems* published by Max Harris in Australia. *The Tree House* published. *Runes* published in England. Four plays performed at Victoria University, Wellington, "James K. Baxter Festival." Commemoration at Christchurch Festival of the Arts.
1974	*The Labyrinth: Some Uncollected Poems 1944 - 1972* published.

Abbreviations

The following abbreviations are used within the text and in the "Notes and References."

Aspects	*Aspects of Poetry in New Zealand*
AT	*Autumn Testament*
BP	*Beyond the Palisade*
BWF	*Blow, Wind of Fruitfulness*
FA	*The Fire and the Anvil*
FC	*The Flowering Cross*
FH	*The Fallen House*
HB	*Howrah Bridge and Other Poems*
IFN	*In Fires of No Return*
JD	*Jerusalem Daybook*
JS	*Jerusalem Sonnets*
MH	*The Man on the Horse*
NS	*The Night Shift*
PIL	*Pig Island Letters*
PU	*Poems Unpleasant*
RW	*The Rock Woman*
Trends	*Recent Trends in New Zealand Poetry*
Weir	J. E. Weir, *The Poetry of James K. Baxter*
Yearbook	*The New Zealand Poetry Yearbook*

CHAPTER 1

Life

WHEN James K. Baxter died suddenly at the age of forty-six in October 1972, New Zealand lost its best known and most significant poet. Moreover, the country was deprived of its one public figure who was a living and vivid example of the full practice of the life of charity, the Christian life. In a span of less than twenty years Baxter had developed from being a boy prodigy of poetry, through days as an alcoholic rip-roarer whose writing became more Freudian the more his social conscience awakened, through further days as Catholic convert and spokesman, to the final few years when he totally rejected urban materialist society and became the figure (barefoot, long-bearded, patched and baggy) whom many saw as saintlike — Hemi, the St. Francis of *nga mokai*, the fatherless, a man who had traveled the path from being something of a disappointing joke to becoming the one who, from his own integration, gave himself wholely. From the youth who asked at eighteen, "What land shall receive me save as a stranger?" he had become at his death a being sure of his community, of his purposes in life, a man widely respected and deeply loved.

More clearly than with many artists, Baxter's life and work are interdependent. From the first a controversial and complex figure, he apparently contained within himself profound contradictions. Deeply moral, he flaunted the conventions of his society over and over again, ignoring social sex taboos, taunting the education system, emphathizing with defeated, decrepit outcasts of the social nexus, finding himself "unable to surrender to the apparently ethical demands of communal utility,"[1] particularly the puritan work ethic and its accompanying material acquisitiveness.

Finding much in New Zealand life to attack, he yet realized that his true personal center was inseparable from his own country, a land whose pioneers, his forebears, "whose bones are in our cemeteries, are the only tribe I know of; and though they were scattered and lost, their unfulfilled intention of charity, peace, and a survival that is more than self-preservation, burns like radium in the cells of my body; and perhaps a fragment of their intention is fulfilled in me, because of my . . . poems that are a permanent sign of contradiction in a world where the pound note and the lens of the analytical Western mind are the only things held sacred" (MH, 12).

Baxter was undoubtedly first and foremost a New Zealander, a necessary condition which he seemed to understand from a very early age. As a child he traveled abroad with his parents; as an adult he visited India and Japan. His whole career shows that he was no limited provincial. His four books of poetry published by Oxford University Press, England, during his lifetime, were widely recognized as the work of a major talent. Presumably, had he been a British or American poet his name would now be much better known. Yet, although one of the finest poets of his generation writing in English, he made virtually no effort to establish a reputation outside the confines of his own small country. This circumstance derives from one of his great strengths, his rootedness in the land and community in which he lived.

Born in Dunedin, southernmost of New Zealand's "four main centers" (i.e., four largest cities), on June 29, 1926, Baxter came of stock which included activist intellectuals on both sides. His maternal grandfather, Professor John MacMillan Brown, who taught English and Classics at the University of Canterbury, became "a legend for his energy, his prejudices, his utopian writings and works on Pacific ethnology, and his part in developing the University of New Zealand."[2] A pioneer in education, one of the shapers of New Zealand society, MacMillan Brown was remembered by his grandson as "a white-haired elderly man in a black coat who inhabited a vast private library."[3] Baxter felt that he and his grandfather would have been uneasy with each other, and yet noted that, "he himself wrote a vigorous satire on his contemporary society, *Riallero;* and in *Limanora* constructed a Utopia where men combined technological progress with moral near-perfection" (FA, 57).

MacMillan Brown's daughter, Baxter's mother, took her B.A. degree at Sydney University and subsequently the Tripos in Modern Languages at Newnham College, Cambridge. On the other side of the family, Baxter's father was a self-educated Otago farmer, with Scottish forebears, a leaning toward Keir Hardie socialism, and strong pacifist convictions. Archibald Baxter had a lifelong habit of reading poetry, and in particular the major English romantic poets — Blake, Shelley, and Byron, and also Burns, Hood, and Henry Lawson. Jim Baxter's early notebooks contain scraps of verse by his father, who is well known in New Zealand for his book *We Will Not Cease: The Autobiography of A Conscientious Objector*, which he wrote in England in 1937, during a family trip to Europe when he also attended the War Resisters' International Conference in Copenhagen.[4]

Among the causes of the "gap . . . simply of difference, between myself and other people," of which Jim Baxter wrote in his own autobiographical sketches, *The Man on the Horse*, he included the contrast of "the closely-knit Otago tribes of my father's family" and the life of John MacMillan Brown in his big house in the Cashmere Hills in Canterbury (which was an English-settled area, as compared to the Scottish Otago to its south). An even greater contrast was the "King and Empire" bellicosity of the general New Zealand population (part of whose small stock of national mythology was the participation of the ANZAC soldiers at Gallipoli) and the socialist pacifism of the Baxter family. Jim Baxter recalled that his father had "suffered almost to the point of death as a conscientious objector in France in the First World War" (MH, 123) and, writing to Maurice Shadbolt in "Pig Island Letters":

> When I was only semen in a gland
> Or less than that, my father hung
> From a torture post at Mud Farm
> Because he would not kill. The guards
> Fried sausages, and as the snow came darkly
> I feared a death by cold in the cold groin
> And plotted revolution. His black and swollen thumbs
> Explained the brotherhood of man. . . .[5]

A quarter of a century later, Terry Baxter, the poet's older brother, was to spend the Second World War in military defaulters' detention camps as a result of his conscientious objection to conscription. Jim Baxter recalls that when he was a teenager, "we could not put on the light in the upper room at night, because . . . neighbours would imagine we were signalling to Japanese submarines" (MH, 123).

As a seven year old, attending school at Brighton, Dunedin, Baxter discovered his vocation as poet, a listener to the music of the universe (the figure is his). He found at once his particular manner of making poems, and its dependence on "the daimon." From the very first day of school he had begun building that resistance to formal education which became typical of him, epitomized in his memory by an occasion when "once in South Canterbury, towards sundown, I went into a deserted one-room country school, and the smell of chalk dust and plasticine and ancient body odours carried with it a piercing message of gloom."[6] From the first he had no wish to learn anything:

> I was already erecting my defences round that core of primitive experience, that ineducable self which I like to call a dinosaur's egg. The abstract analytical processes which the schools were prepared to offer me, and ram down my throat, if necessary . . . have the side effect of neutralizing this kind of experience and making it inaccessible to the conscious mind. The two types of learning were opposed; the first being the discovery of a sacred pattern in natural events; the second being the acquisition of the lens of abstract thought which sees nothing sacred on the face of the earth.

Not long after Jim started school his family moved to the North Island and for a year he attended the Quaker School on St. John's Hill, Wanganui; but he afterward felt that for him true learning occurred in the immediate neighborhood of his house, in a thick-bushed gully with a little stream running through it, or at the sea beach or Virginia Lake, from which came some of his most effective early poems ("The Bay," "Virginia Lake"). The school's punishment system, an arrangement whereby the child recorded his own misdemeanors and carried the record with him, taught Baxter "a kind of impenitent despair."

When his family shifted to England in 1937 Jim was again sent to a Quaker school, this time a boarding school in the Cotswolds. Again there was a positive side, a rich firsthand experience of nature, particularly bird life, and the learning of nature lore, but inevitably there continued the betrayal of childhood innocence, the harsh opening of the way into the adult world:

> I touch them with a word, so close they stand
> After a thousand hours and days,
> Older than Cocteau, in the dream museum
> Of corridors and changing rooms;
> A palace, jail and maze.
>
> There I imbibed, as at a breast, truth
> Beside the simple streams and elms;

Life

> England my wet nurse, with her bitter milk.
> So from sugared childhood came
> On to the watershed of tears
> With those small angular companions,
> Handlers of the penis and the pen.
>
> Hard to forgive them even now,
> Precursors of the adult nightmare —
> Franey, Nero of the dormitory,
> Holmes, with the habits of a jaguar
> And the sleek animal hide,
> Waiting in a bend of the high stone stair.
>
> Plunged early into the abyss of life
> Where the tormentors move,
> At war with God, the terrible Watcher,
> An octopus behind a round glass window
> With knives and justice, but no love.
>
> That guilt grew wrongly, driven underground
> With the first prickings of raw sense.
> Yet there was friendship, comics, dominoes,
> A dried newt like a bootsole in a drain,
> New conkers like peeled testicles,
> Sharing of exile, and the habit, pain.
>
> The village like a mother stayed outside
> With wells and horses, till the coat
> Of manhood could be stitched and worn —
> And the green mandrake, Poetry,
> Born whole and shrieking one bleak night
> Under stiff sheets and wincing at the dawn.[7]

Wrenched out of childhood by the vinegared teats of his "wet nurse," England, Baxter was now "born whole" as a poet and from this time on, particularly upon his return to New Zealand and a further year at St. John's, Wanganui, he wrote poems copiously and regularly. From Wanganui in 1940 he returned to Dunedin and was enrolled in King's High School, where his parents kept him out of the military cadets, an organization which, he observed, had an imprisoning effect on the other boys. "Their faces became wooden and their language monotonous. They were entering the borders of the collective fantasy generated by Ares, dealer in souls. My own fantasies were Venusian, perhaps less harmful" (MH, 137). His unwillingness to learn, school-formula fashion, never deserted him, but the dinosaur's egg had begun to hatch. He had begun to cross "the authentic and terrible grey rock desert of adolescence," feeling vulnerable to pressures "to accept the Calvinist ethos which underlies our determinedly secular culture . . . *work is good; sex is evil; do what you're told and you'll be all right; don't dig too deep into yourself"* (MH, 125), seeing himself as:

> I, in my fuggy room at the top of the stairs,
> A thirteen-year-old schizophrene,
> Write poems, wish to die,
> And watch the long neat mason-fly
> Malignantly serene
> Arrive with spiders dopier than my mind
> And build his clay dungeons inside the roller blind.
> (MH, 127)

During this whole period he was developing his craft of verse: for instance, he tells in *The Fire & The Anvil* (p. 16) of his discovery of stress rhythms. He left King's High School at the end of 1943 and enrolled as an arts student at Otago University, but he dropped out after a year or so, having discovered that "Aphrodite, Bacchus and the Holy Spirit were my tutors, but the goddess of good manners and examination passes withheld her smile from me."[8] He has written movingly of this period in *Pig Island Letters:*

> At seventeen I thought I might see
> Not fire but water rise
>
> From the shelves of surf beyond St. Clair
> To clang the dry bell. Gripping
> A pillow wife in bed
> I did my convict drill,
> And when I made a mother of the keg
> The town split open like an owl's egg
> Breaking the ladders down. It was
> Perhaps the winter of beginning:
>
> Frost standing up like stubble in the streets
> Below the knees of Maori Hill
> Looking for the last simplicity
> And nothing to explain it in the books,

Life

> In a room where the wind clattered the blind-cord
> In the bed of a girl with long plaits
> I found the point of entry
> The place where father Adam died.
>
> Meanwhile a boy with dog and ferret
> Climbed up the gorse track from the sea
> To the turn at the top of the gully
> Twelve paces past the cabbage tree,
> And saw from the crest of the hill
> Pillars of rain move on the dark sea,
> A cloud of fire rise up above Japan,
> God's body blazing on damnation's tree.

He concluded, as he said in lecture at Auckland University in 1963, that any individual who survived intact a British type of education "would feel at home anywhere — in a space ship going to Venus or a pit full of tarantulas."

John Lehmann's *New Writing*, Jung's *Modern Man in Search of a Soul*, the educational ideas and writings of A. S. Neill, and "a sloppily written anarchist tract by Ethel Mannin, called *Bread and Roses*" (MH, 127) were influences on Baxter's intellectual life at this time. He felt a link, of attitude and approach, between the leftist British poets (by which he meant Auden, Spender, Day Lewis, and MacNeice) and Australian balladists such as Henry Lawson and Banjo Paterson, but he was unaware of the work of other New Zealand poets until 1944, the year in which the Caxton Press published his first volume of poems, *Beyond the Palisade*. That year he wrote to A. R. D. Fairburn, with the result that they exchanged epigrams, and Fairburn, characteristically, offered the young Baxter advice about the conduct of his sex life which, characteristically, was not taken.

At nineteen, in Dunedin, he worked in a rolling mill at Green Island, living in digs, free for the first time (apart from the oppressions of boarding school) from close family contact. Looking back, he saw that time as an indolent lull:

> Delighting him, who for the moment had
> Money, a mistress, all that the young require
> To walk Niagara. . . .
>   Indeed he seemd to lie
> Masterless at length in the good centre
> Of nineteen years' maze, the green boy come of age —

Not seeing the handsized cloud in the clear sky
And the door ajar to let the Furies enter.[9]

Not long after this, he had an apparently unsatisfactory first contact with Charles Brasch, a poet who had returned to New Zealand after spending the war years in Britain. Brasch was very shortly to found *Landfall*, which during the 1950s and 1960s was a focus of intellectual life and is the most influential literary magazine New Zealand has had.

By 1948, having for the moment at least given up university study, Baxter had moved north to Christchurch, home territory of his notable grandfather. Here the young poet met two other key figures of the 1930s group, Denis Glover, a force both as poet and printer, and Allen Curnow, a journalist who was also an able poet and influential critic:

> The true town will evade your map,
> Murderous, choked by its cathedral stone.
> Those granite jowls I remember,
> A.'s hornet nest of Yeatsian prose,
>
> D. flattened in a chair, dead drunk on gin,
> A vague fog rising from the Avon,
> A city founded in wanhope
> And English, English, English to the bone.[10]

Thus Baxter saw Christchurch and its chief ornaments of poetry in 1948. If he could identify with Glover in terms of common human problems, he shared with Curnow some area of intellectual concern. Curnow eventually became a notable teacher of Yeats, and Yeats was a prime influence on Baxter's poetry of the late 1940s and early 1950s. (Baxter was adept at using other poets as models.) Over the years the relationship between Curnow and Baxter remained ambivalent. To begin with, Curnow as editor was generous to Baxter, seeing in him the chief hope for the future of poetry in New Zealand. But already in the early 1950s Baxter questioned Curnow's judgments and by the period 1956 - 59, when the controversial *Penguin Book of New Zealand Verse* was being shaped and reshaped, Curnow's affirmations had given way to a tendency to minimize Baxter's talent, so that the anthology contains ten pages of Baxter's work (which Weir, for example, calls an "unbalanced representation")[11] and two pages of largely unfavorable critical comment upon it. The rift between the two poets was part of a larger squabble, between Curnow and the whole group of younger poets who lived in Wellington in the mid and late 1950s. Since Curnow and Baxter are perhaps the two most influential figures in New Zealand poetry up to the present time, their relationship was of some significance.

In contrast, during the same period some kind of common understanding existed between Baxter and Glover, presumably deriving in part from each man's troublesome private colloquy with Bacchus. Baxter has said to the present writer that he and Glover did not much discuss the craft of verse, but that he "had never met a man who was more aware of his own destitution." Elsewhere, discussing influences on his work and the development of his technique, he says that he learned something from Glover of how to write sparely, in "sessions . . . conducted in the Gladstone Hotel, where Glover's contemplative powers had their full flowering."[12] A section of *The Man on the Horse* conveys vividly the texture of Baxter's life at this time:

> I had been looking for a job for ten days. At that time I was living on my own in a shack beside a garage behind an old boarding house in a suburb of Christchurch. A little dog-kennel of a place with a stretcher, a gas ring, a chest of drawers and a ripped gas-light on a pipe from the ceiling. Sometimes I wanted to plug up the door and turn on the gas without lighting it, but other times, especially on a fine morning, you could see hundreds of wax-eyes swinging on the sow-thistle heads outside. It was only eight bob a week, and that meant freedom as I saw it then — to work or not to work, to come home as late as I liked, to put into words the shape of the world inside me (though I never managed that) — and of course to get drunk. There was a girl who came to see me pretty often, but I don't think she liked the place as well as I did.
>
> The job I'd been in before had lasted three days. It was a job grinding brass taps. You wore gloves, but the brass dust and the emery wheel wore through the gloves, and they didn't supply new ones just for the asking. I had been drinking a lot the week before I took the job on, and the cold weather and the brass dust made me feel worse instead of better. So when the foreman said I was bloody useless, perhaps he was in the right for once. All the same, it wasn't the kind of job anyone would stay at for long.
>
> The money from that job kept me going for a couple of days. And when it was gone, the milkman still left two bottles at the door of the shack every morning. I would sleep till the early afternoon. It was very quiet in the afternoon, almost as if the world had ended and everyone else had died. Every day I'd pour the milk, pure and white and cold, into a grimy glass I'd

pinched from a pub somewhere, and gulp it down, and go out into the hardworking city afternoon to look for another job. But no one needed a young man with a stubble and an overcoat and a look of not quite belonging — not the gasworks, nor the wet timber yard, nor the boot factory that only employed girls, and least of all the Employment Bureau. So I'd buy an apple and go into Hagley Park to look at the swans. A lot of things worried me then that wouldn't worry me now in the same way — God, and sex, and the old men like broken-down horses who polished brass taps and sat in a corner of the pub saying nothing, and the high pale clouds over the park trees. It seemed to me the world couldn't go on the way it was going. There was a secret switch, almost within reach of anyone's hand, that would change the raw, tangled lives in a moment to real love and creative joy. The park trees promised it. The swans ruffled their feathers on the slaty, ruffled water. (151 - 53)

Blow, Wind of Fruitfulness, Baxter's second book, was published during this Christchurch year. Written between 1945 and 1948, the poems were composed while he worked as a farm laborer, freezing worker, sanitarium porter, foundryman, mail carrier, bellhop, and proofreader for a newspaper. When, at the end of 1948, he married Jacqueline Sturm and moved north again, to Wellington, he took a job at the Wellington meat-freezing works and resumed some measure of university work, taking a course in Greek History, Art and Literature extramurally from Victoria University College.

For most of the next seventeen years he lived in Wellington, where his two children, Hilary and John, were born. He worked at a variety of jobs and was even, at one point or another, tempted to enter academic life. As a part-time student in the early and mid-1950s he gradually completed a B.A. degree, finding particularly irksome the Anglo-Saxon and Middle English sections of the English major. From the freezing works he went back to carrying mail for a year after which he enrolled at Wellington Teachers' Training College, then the most forward-looking of the New Zealand colleges. When he was awarded his Teaching Certificate he taught elementary school, but was never happy or comfortable purveying an "education" which he had rejected with his whole being when on the receiving end of the process. Before too long he found what seemed a more appropriate occupation as a subeditor in the School Publications branch of the Education Department. Another accomplished New Zealand poet, Alistair Campbell, also worked for School Publications, which, then as now, had the most adventurous and judiciously crafted program of its kind (publication of "monographs" and quarterly bulletins for all age levels) anywhere in the world. Baxter, however, was never particularly at ease in the job and was irritated by his forced participation in the educational bureaucracy. He remained reluctantly until 1962 when he returned to mail carrying; he was later to become a mail sorter.

During the 1950s many of the most important developments in his life were, probably, his first efforts to deal with his alcoholism. Early in the decade he had a reputation as a "soak," and some of his finest, most humane writing (such as his "Lament for Barney Flanagan") arises from that condition. A fellow writer later to be associated with Baxter in editing the literary magazine *Numbers*, tells of an incident characteristic of the period:

> Going along Taranaki Street one winter evening I saw this small crowd gathered near the Hong Kong cafe and from the midst of it came the sound of a deep, rich voice shouting "Milton!" I went over and there was Jim lying on the pavement apparently invoking the spirit of the old Puritan poet. Instead, it was Louis Johnson who emerged from the Hong Kong cafe. He helped Baxter up and they went off together towards Newtown.
> . . . this whole scene in the lamplit darkness had, for me, an heroic quality. It made me feel the presence of poetry even in the streets of Wellington, a possibility which at that time I was not otherwise disposed to believe in. Nor was the incident spoilt for me, in fact I suppose it became richer, when I realized many years later that the Milton who was being called upon was not the poet but (was) a friend of Baxter's (who had that day come out of jail).[13]

Not long after this Baxter made contact with Alcoholics Anonymous and soon became a concerned and active member.

Louis Johnson and Baxter developed a close friendship and literary association, which proved fruitful for them both throughout the 1950s and somewhat beyond. Johnson, and not Baxter, became a gathering point in Wellington for the life of poetry. His first effective book, *The Sun Among the Ruins*, was published in 1951, and throughout the decade he also edited *The New Zealand Poetry Yearbook*. By vocation a poet, Johnson was by profession a journalist. Where Baxter was at that time a rather fugitive and erratic personality, Johnson was available to all young writers, especially those who aspired to become poets, and a good number of writers owe him a debt of gratitude for his having helped them to develop. Openly and bitingly critical of the social and moral attitudes of New Zealand society, he was less polished but no less perceptive than Baxter, who once said of him, "It was the sense of being in the lion's den which he could give shape to."[14] Baxter admired a Rabelaisian wit and an engaging Dionysian quality in Johnson, which had counterparts in his own personality. Adopting an iconoclastic stance, the two gave each other support, and when, over the years, a growing chorus of academic critics attacked Johnson's work, Baxter felt that the criticism was either irrelevant or due to bafflement "by a new mode of thought, feeling and language — one could almost say, a new dimension of reality approached and recognized."[15] Johnson and Baxter shared a mythologizing tendency and a fruitful interest in the writings of Freud and Jung. Baxter's progressively deepening commitment to social causes may well have owed something to Johnson's persistent belief that poetry could and should be used as a weapon in the war against social ills and injustices. The two men's friendship resulted in the collaborative books *Poems Unpleasant* (1952) and *The Night Shift* (1957) and in the publication of the Wellington magazine *Numbers* (1954 - 59). No extended comment on the relationship has yet been published by either writer, but it is perhaps the most interesting one to occur so far in New Zealand writing. Each man, from time to time, continued to publish comments (in reviews, etc.) on the other, but indications are that the main impetus of the relationship was over when Johnson left Wellington for Hawke's Bay in the mid-1960s. Already by then Baxter had addressed to Johnson a moving poem which has a valedictory air:

> 'The icy dawn of the sixties' —
> Yes, you have it there.
> Today I saw a black sperm whale
> Rolled on the rocks at Pukerua Bay.
>
> The stench grew loud as I came near,
> Gulls were grabbing at the kill.
> From that sleek projectile body
> Jutted a gigantic reddened phallus
> Mauled by the Cook Strait squid.
>
> Under the sunset fires it seemed to be
> The body of our common love
> That bedrooms, bar rooms never killed,
> The natural power behind our acts and verses
> Murdered by triviality.
>
> (HB, 55)

Indications throughout Baxter's writings, at every stage, suggest that he was naturally disposed to a belief in God, and that for him the Christian religion was a matter of serious concern. For a time in the 1950s, he was involved in the Anglican communion. In 1951 he attended classes in first-year philosophy at Victoria University College. That same year the Department of Philosophy acquired a new Head, Professor George Hughes, who was also an Anglican minister. Baxter came to know Hughes, and was, for a period, a member of his congregation; but by the midfifties, possibly under the double influence of the doctrine of the Real Presence and of his feeling for the Blessed Virgin, who is "in charge of all supernatural communications," Baxter evinced a growing interest in Roman Catholicism. He began to attend Masses at St. Mary's Basilica, Boulcott Street, Wellington, and in 1958 was formally received into the Catholic Church.

A God-conscious individual, he was also aware of the inevitable struggle between the artist's creative freedom and church authority. He wrote to John Weir that his conversion was "founded on the natural ground of that utter lack of credulity, that abyss of scepticism which makes me call myself a modern man."[16] In *The Man on the Horse* he connects the conversion explicitly with a derelict rum-soak whom he calls Seamas, a man troubled in every phase of his existence but who "had no religious trouble whatever." Baxter comments that "he taught me that belief, not virtue, was the entrance ticket at the door of the Church" (MH, 45). Baxter's inner condition he himself saw as one of destitution, similar to the "impenitent despair" of his schooldays. Despite his independence as an artist, he showed considerable self-discipline from then on in his view of the church and his capacity for understanding its directives. A vivid image from that time illuminates:

> Image of the soul: a granary
> Moon-blind, inhabited by hungry rats;
> Or those great fish that nudge
> For rice grains on a sluggish pond
> Whose freshet lies outside itself.[17]

At any rate, from the time of his conversion onward Baxter became a leading and valued spokesman for the Catholic Church in New Zealand and his church involvement led ultimately to the final phase of social activism.

A UNESCO-sponsored trip to India in the latter part of 1958 obviously further stirred Baxter's social conscience. His experiences yielded two articles in *Education* in 1959 and 1960 (and a later tribute to Rabindranath Tagore), plus a handful of poems and the title of his book *Howrah Bridge and Other Poems*. Darkly vivid as they are, the collection of India poems are not technically different from other work in the volume, which shows the influence, both in a loosening of the line and in a particularity of observation, of a close reading of the British poet Lawrence Durrell.

In India Baxter observed another version of the gap between the bureaucratic idea of education and the depth of indigenous culture: "The Indian educationist rarely recognizes that literacy and education are not co-terminous. In the communal life of her villages, India already possesses a constant cultural reservoir, independent of schools and book learning, which New Zealand, for example, has never had."[18] He learned, too, about the integrity of each distinctive Indian village community, and presumably this had an effect on his final phase at Jerusalem.

Meanwhile, he had become increasingly restive in his subediting work at School Publications (in a letter to the present writer 28 June 1963, he refers to "the educational boa constrictor that moistens you so lovingly before it swallows you"), finding it difficult if not impossible to meet deadlines for the bulletins assigned to him. Relinquishing the job in 1962, he went back to the post office, remaining there until the end of 1965, when he returned to Dunedin. After 1961, the year in which he collaborated in a "coffee-table" publication entitled *New Zealand in Colour*, there was, during the early 1960s, a falling-off in the quantity of work he published. The period is marked by no major book publication, although his play *The Wide Open Cage*, which had had "the most ecstatic press of any New Zealand play to date"[19] when it was performed locally in 1959, had a brief run in New York City in 1962.

Late in 1965, Baxter was awarded a Robert Burns Fellowship, which took him back to the University of Otago, initially to spend a year there, giving an occasional lecture but chiefly writing. Among his plans was a proposal to "work on the memoirs of my grandfather, John MacMillan Brown." Writing in *The Dominion* on 23 October 1965, Louis Johnson suggested that, "the Burns scholarship may well mark a turning-point in his career."[20] Johnson was referring to a tendency then not uncommon among New Zealand artists for their careers to falter when they were in their late thirties or thereabouts, and was suggesting that the opportunity to devote a year fully to writing (after years of trudging the Wellington hills with a mailbag slung on his shoulder) would carry Baxter through such a potential crisis and give his career fresh impulse. From that time, in fact, Bax-

Life 33

ter did seem to have a new store of energy, but not perhaps of the kind Johnson imagined. In the late 1960s, Baxter's life was to take an not-altogether-expected turn.

While he was still in Wellington in 1963 he wrote "The Landward Farms" (for the novelist Maurice Shadbolt), a poem which derived from Baxter's sense of "that profoundly negative fury symbolized in the coastal weather"[21] of Otago, of which he was conscious from his earliest years. Thus began the title-sequence of *Pig Island Letters*, published in 1966, his first year back in Dunedin. Garnering Baxter's second Jessie Mackay Memorial Award, the book also marks the beginning of his last phase of publication.

He took the task of offering some set Fellowship lectures seriously and produced *Aspects of New Zealand Poetry* (1967), plus a small book of poems, *The Lion Skin* (1967), and a rich collage of autobiographical materials, some dating back to the early 1950's, *The Man on the Horse* (1967). His Burns Fellowship was extended for a year and his play *The Spots of the Leopard* was produced at the Downstage Theatre in Wellington, and also in New York where it was ill-received by the critics. Baxter was now launched as a playwright, particularly through the interest and friendship of Patric Carey, whose Globe Theatre produced seven Baxter plays, including *The Band Rotunda*, *The Sore-Footed Man*, *The Bureaucrat*, and *The Devil and Mr. Mulcahy* in 1967 and 1968, and staged a Baxter Festival. Carey mounted the first production of Baxter's *Temptations of Oedipus* in 1970.

Two years as Burns Fellow were followed by a further year in Dunedin in which Baxter participated in catechetical work, meantime writing a series of religious articles for the *New Zealand Tablet*, which were later published as *The Flowering Cross* in 1969, in which year he moved north to Auckland, where he helped to establish a Narcotics Anonymous group. *The Rock Woman*, his selected poems, was also published then. That same year, Baxter suffered an "identity crisis," (so termed by the *Dominion* newspaper), which resulted in his leaving his family in Wellington and taking to the road.

Living at first alone, he fetched up at a tiny settlement on the Wanganui River, called Jerusalem. Presumably he was attracted to it, as he had been drawn to Hawke's Bay some years earlier, because it was a Catholic settlement. An old Catholic mission, by this time Jerusalem was a dying bush town, and Baxter found quarters in a disused, broken-down unfurnished cottage hidden among rank grass and ancient, lichen-dripping walnut trees. To a reporter in 1970 he described the local community as "a very small Maori village. About 25 people, or thereabouts. But they accept me. I'm not encroaching. Maoris are brothers, you see. It's a heritage we're trying to take from them. . . ."[22]

To this community he next added a group, varying in numbers, of social drop-outs, people seeking refuge from the police, from their families, from a variety of problems. From being a solitary he had become a "patriarch" for these people, himself envisaging among them a possible "future as a mutually supporting community of souls." Never a man to whom small practical matters came easily, he now began in rough and ready fashion to grow his own food and to lend support to the community by means of what little money he could make in writing for newspapers and periodicals. Living conditions were spartan in the extreme and food nearly always scarce, depending as it did on donations, Baxter's slim money supply, and whatever was earned through the casual labor of one or other member of the group. Baxter himself had taken a vow of total poverty, a step thoroughly consistent with his lifelong attitudes to materialism, and it was the nature of this condition which occupied much of his thinking and writing in the last two years or so of his life. From being "James K. Baxter" he became Hemi (Maori equivalent of James), very conscious of Maori language and customs, as is evident from all his writing published in the 1970s.

Close contact with the unemployed in Auckland (a small group, since New Zealand normally has a very low rate of unemployment) put him in touch with what his soul had long sought for, a genuine community. "They worried about each other," he told the reporter Barrie Watts, "helped each other, and shared what they could when it was needed. If one had food they all had food. If one had a dollar they all had a dollar."[23] For years he, like Louis Johnson, had been critical of the emptiness, loneliness, and mental ill engendered by suburban life and the "nuclear" family. As a consequence of the deeply felt contrast between the sterility of mass society and his experiences of common charity among the deprived, Baxter, in Watts' words, "set out almost ritualistically on a private odyssey. He arrived at Jerusalem." The place appealed to him because it was Catholic and Maori and cut off from the supermarket and subdivision culture which was overtaking New Zealand. "Maoris know how to live together," he said. "They practise the bigger collective unity principle. It's highly civilized. That's the essence of the *marae* system, and it's why individual Maoris become so easily lost when they move away from it into the cities and towns."

Life 35

For New Zealand even, where the practice of living in simple solitude in the bush or on a remote beach is not altogether uncommon, this community of souls was remarkable. The settlement itself was difficult to reach, being accessible only by river or by unpaved back roads; it was many miles away from the nearest main road and twenty-five miles from the small town of Raetihi. But in Baxter's first six months there, some 150 people came to see him, with up to ten staying with him at any one time, bunking on bare boards. Baxter himself, the mentor, had by the end of 1970 come to have an inward, rabbinical look; but the complexities of his character remained. As one reporter put it (and by this time Baxter and his commune were being written about constantly in New Zealand magazines and newspapers): "At times his speech is deeply spiritual and gentle, but in a flicker he becomes crude with the tongue of a worker who has dropped a hammer on his toe."[24] Pervaded by spirituality as they are, his last writings continue to manifest such apparent contradictions. But they may be more apparent than real. Baxter had always been this kind of mixture, and at the end, many would say, his life was an integrated whole, the meeting of *yin* and *yang*.

Despite his hopes to the contrary and his unwillingness to buy the land at Jerusalem away from the Maoris, partly because of his belief in their birthright and partly because of his own vow of poverty, Baxter found that by mid-1971 the Jerusalem community was under attack from the Maori landowners who feared that the area would get a reputation which would make young Maoris unwilling to commit themselves to settling there. Pressure against the Baxter "family" came also from another quarter, the Wanganui County Council, which in March 1971 had laid down conditions that facilities, particularly for sanitation, must be improved at Jerusalem. Baxter welcomed some of the suggestions, believing that they would prompt the members of his community into some kind of practical action, but he also declared: "If the local Maoris want me to shift, I'll leave tomorrow. If anyone else does, they'd better bring up a helicopter to get me out."[25] In the event the Maoris themselves had come to the conclusion that the Jerusalem community was a degradation of Maoritanga. By the (southern) spring of 1971 the communal experiment at Jerusalem seemed to be over and Baxter had returned to his family at Wellington.

During that period of the Jerusalem experiment Baxter continued to write and publish. *Jerusalem Sonnets* (1970) won for him a third Jessie Mackay Award. Four of the plays which had been produced so successfully by Patric Carey at the Globe were published in two volumes by Heinemann in 1971, in which year also appeared *Jerusalem Daybook*, a journal of mixed prose and verse. Formally this was to be the final stage in the development of Baxter's writing.

Very shortly after the Jerusalem commune had closed down, a newspaper report suggested that the local Maoris had relented and would welcome Baxter's return.[26] The same report concluded that "he hopes he will be buried in Jerusalem." (Baxter apparently felt that he had not long to live for in the early months of 1972, although he had accepted an invitation to participate in the 1973 Christchurch Arts Festival, he told a Christchurch acquaintance that he would not see him again.)[27] Late in 1971, however, he was involved in the day-to-day affairs of an urban commune at MacDonald Crescent, Wellington. This apparently started shortly after the closure of Jerusalem, and again Baxter was the central figure, to whom others turned for love and advice, protection from the threat of jail or mental hospital. At Christmas 1971, he told the present writer that he would wish to return to Jerusalem, but with far fewer people, a small "family." For a short period he did this, but within a year he was dead, of a heart attack or malnutrition. At forty-six an unusual, many-sided life was over. By this time he had become a national legend, so that memorial services in Auckland and Wellington were heavily attended, and reporters and cameramen mingled with the 800 mourners at the Jerusalem burial, an emotional scene of witness and testimony to the strong feelings many held for the dead poet. Maori hymns and orations were a spontaneous part of the occasion and even the traditional *haka* when Baxter's mother was received on the *marae*.

Most of the last months of Baxter's life were apparently spent in the Grafton "community" in Auckland, where he died. He continued to write, and the work continued to be published: *Ode to Auckland and Other Poems* (1972), *Letter to Peter Olds* (1972, two impressions), *Autumn Testament* (1972, reprinted 1973). The title poem of this last work, a forty-eight-section sequence, may well prove to be his finest achievement in writing.

CHAPTER 2

The Early Poetry

I believe a new and valuable stereotype is in process of being formed: the view of national history held by the poet who has grown up in entire acceptance of his environment, truly inhabiting the country.[1]

AMONG the Baxter papers in the Hocken Library, Dunedin, is a shelf of black-covered notebooks which one remembers seeing twenty years ago or more in the Baxters' house in Wilton Road, Wellington. These are the faithful record of a very young apprenticeship. Baxter himself has told us that he wrote his first poem when he was seven years old. The earliest dated poem in the notebooks is a Poe-like piece entitled "Satan's Battle," inscribed when Baxter was eleven. All eighty-three poems in this first notebook were written before he was fourteen. Pastiche, the work is done with remarkable sureness and competence. In character, much of it is nature verse and there is evidence of the pacifism for which father and brother paid dearly in each of the World Wars.

While the first eleven notebooks show the poet mastering his formal means in fluent, accurate imitation of various modes and models, quite obviously the genuine spark is there and, in notebook 12, shows distinct signs of a growing flexibility in management of measure and line. One ten-page piece of practice metrics entitled "Bird-Envocation" *(sic)* is dismissed at the conclusion as "Just a piece of neo-Skeltonian fantasia," but it is skillfully done, and the poem following it, "Love Lyric, II" (complete with Hopkins-like notations) provides evidence of a good ear and an ability to compress:

> The barbed secretive whip of anger flaying
> I watch the winds on the hill-shoulder and shore;
> mist like smoke from fires over paper pastures

floating; rain-sodden stacks; and across the gully, toy sheep. . . .

One hundred sixteen pages of this notebook were filled in February - March 1944 (including a Victor Hugo translation and a "found poem") with the material of a crucial stage in Baxter's grappling with both technical problems and those of relating his own personal experience to the larger moral abstractions. Dante, Burns, Tolstoi, Meredith, Emily Bronte, Byron, Rimbaud, and Yeats are referred to, and notebook 10 includes many imitations of Hopkins and one of William Empson. Notebook 13 reveals an extensive engagement with the craft of the short line, sometimes used to gnomic effect. Time and season (of an internal landscape), death, the traditional hunger for immortality of the artist are Baxter's thematic preoccupations. One poem, "In July" (1944) is deployed in Audenesque eight-line stanzas and refers to "Auden my master," but is followed immediately by the un-Auden-like "Death of a Swan." Most of notebook 14 is influenced by Auden, though its later pages are under the sway of Dylan Thomas (this was in 1946, when Baxter was nineteen or twenty, the year in which Thomas' *Death and Entrances* was published).

I   Beyond the Palisade

Many key poems of Baxter's first volume, *Beyond the Palisade*,[2] were written by the time he was seventeen, and fair copies may be found in notebooks 10 - 13, a substantial number in notebook 10. Work contained in this and later notebooks has a greater range both in substance and technique, than is revealed in *Beyond the Palisade*. Available to him was a considerably larger collection, looser and more colloquial in texture; the making of the book was a considerable act of self-criticism and self-shaping.

As it is, *Beyond the Palisade* displays versatility in polished use of short-lined quatrains and longer, more ruminative forms. Its themes include the force of nature ("Eagle"); nature's cruelty and menace on this "immense/ And hump-backed planet"; man's cruelty within nature ("The Killing of a Rabbit"); nature versus man ("The Mountains", which "crouch like tigers"); a kind of vague despair — "me upon a waiting Ararat:/ (The flood may not subside)"; the fate of all living creatures which "Are born, beget and die"; the difference between Maori and *pakeha* (white settler) in terms of belonging to the land, the poverty of *pakeha* existence in relation to it, and the

The Early Poetry

consequent poverty of *pakeha* history. Dominating the whole book is a sense of isolated man in the clutch of mortality and cruel, indifferent nature, of men who "shut within a whelming bowl of hills/ Grow strange" for

> A sense as of vast fate rings in the blood; no refuge
> No refuge is there from the flame that reaches
>
> Among familiar things and makes them seem
> Trivial, vain.
> (BP, 9, "The Mountains")

This flame is not part of the natural scene, but part of Baxter's inner landscape which overlays it, and it may be glossed by "Fire in the Mountains" (p. 27); "Run, boys, run: the fire is a master," and illuminated by Baxter's passing comment of approval on MacNeice's "Brother Fire" a poem which addresses "dialectician Fire, O enemy and image of ourselves" (FA, 21), and Baxter's early declaration that "Animism is an essential factor in the artist's view of the world" (*Trends*, 7).

Similarly, especially in the early poetry, the wind carries a burden of suggestiveness, usually either premonitory or cleansing ("Wind of dissolution, wind of creation"). In "Love Lyric, IV" (BP, 25):

> There is a distant roaring of wind
> lulling and rising
> in quiet night,

the "quiet night" being, in a Jungian sense, the unconscious:

> Each man who looks on the night
> creates or destroys
> creates and destroys himself therein.

Man must "look on" his unconscious and perceive it clearly before he can bring it into full relationship with consciousness, so achieving personal integration. Despite the vast differences of nurture and culture, the quality of what is seen in the dark of the unconscious is in no way necessarily different for modern man than "for the aborigines," and the "night-universe," existing at a depth which is ampler and more all-embracing, "surpasses reason." Not that Baxter was already consciously Jungian, but his sense of inner experience had a naturally Jungian tendency and some fragments of "Love Lyric, IV" are an early manifestation of it.

Baxter's portrayal of the Otago landscape, darker than the actuality, is expressionistic, giving substance to feelings of nihilism and determinism. Recurring images of cloud, wind, cold, the pervasive aura of doom-laden emptiness — these are what he made of "the bare coast between Dunedin and Taieri Mouth," the place where he first encountered "the gap, the void" which caused him to "break out in words":

> After reading The Heroes of Asgard, I described
> it in a very early piece of verse —
>
>> Long, long ago, ere e'en the world was made,
>> Was naught but chaos, the abyss of space,
>> The deep Ginungagap — on one side lay
>> Cold Niflheim, home of frosts and gloomy mists
>> And in it was the cauldron Hvergelmir,
>> The source of twelve great rivers of strange waves
>> That flowed into the space and chaos far
>> To freeze therein; while to the south there was
>> The red abode of Muspellheim,
>> The glowing home of the eternal fires. . . .
>
> (MH, 122 - 23)

This fragment of juvenilia, presumably part of a longer piece which may not now be extant, prefaces his explanation of his sense of a gap between himself and other people. Inhabitants of middle-earth, they, unlike him, live unaware of the abyss or the world-mist and the eternal fires. He, on the other hand, saw his native landscape as part of a larger reality. As he once said: "What happens is either meaningless to me, or else it is mythology" (MH, 122).

Otherwise, he apparently chose to confine his selection for his first published book so that it centered on New Zealand. From the notebooks he could have taken work concerned with war in Europe, or containing references to Van Gogh, El Greco, Napoleon, etc. — poems which (leaving aside the question of merit) would have given the book a different aura, a larger and more outward-looking perspective. Absent from *Beyond the Palisade* but present here and there in the notebooks is a certain lack of reverence, an attitude which was to prove so fruitful in Baxter's maturity. In 1944 he might

The Early Poetry

not, perhaps, have made a better book, but he could have produced one equally competent and yet not so pervasively solemn as the one we have. Yet, reading both sets of material, one is convinced that right instinct led to his limiting of focus, refusing the easy light, attaching himself instead to a small group of symbols which grasp, intuitively, a New Zealand still empty of man; the coming of the Polynesian voyagers, "people who fought against the aboriginal New Zealand demon with their own crude spiritual weapons";[3] the *pakeha* pioneers with their doomed dream of the Just City. To the end of his life and with ever-deepening commitment, Baxter believed in the need for the tribe, attributing the desperate state of society to the destruction of "the stubborn clans" and man's failure to rebuild them. In this respect he anticipated the work and attitudes of Gary Snyder and others. Over twenty years ago he stated simultaneously his belief in the tradition and his ense of the possibilities of human contact. Thinking of his forebears, he said: "The peasant clansmen of the Western Highlands of Scotland became the clannish farmers of Otago. The Otago Hills and seacoast are not unlike the hills and seacoast of Argyllshire. So I have been fortunate enough to find the ready-made myth of longbearded Gaelic-speaking giants distilling whisky among the flax from time immemorial. The ancestral face is very familiar to me". (*Trends*, 7). From an early stage his work shows signs of his longing for a positive human community.

II Blow, Wind of Fruitfulness

Two books, *Blow, Wind of Fruitfulness* (1948) and its successor *The Fallen House* (1953), established Baxter's reputation as a poet and, together with his address to the New Zealand Writers' Conference in Christchurch in 1951 (published as *Recent Trends in New Zealand Poetry*), made him, in his midtwenties, a key figure. As early as 1945 Allen Curnow had written of him, "strong in impulse and confident in invention . . . since Mason in 1923, no New Zealand poet has proved so early his power to say and his right to speak."[4] Within a very few years Baxter was to astonish with the lyric elegance and grace of much of his work, so that in later years critics coping with the jagged, spiky poems of the 1960s showed at first a tendency to hark back to the mellifluous sweetness of the early work. Writing in *New Zealand Poetry Yearbook* in 1954 Baxter reveals something of his attitude then; to be a poet, "a cell of good living in a corrupt society," was vocation enough.

> Should we take rhetoric and wring its neck? Yes, if what is meant is the ornamental clichés of a poem, the dead wood. Pruning is a poet's main job anyway. But if you mean the *time-life* of a poem, its existence as a rhythmical sensory pattern in time — by no means, it can't be done. Rhetoric is an emotionally coloured term. It may mean ossified formal language; or a poet's method which is directed to words as an effective audible pattern in their own right. Even the best verbal pattern can only be a vehicle, a reflection of the core or matrix of a poem, that unwritten mystery which it is wrapped around. But if you deny the poet the right to play building blocks with words, you will not get poems but only animal noises.[5]

He was to travel a long way from these circumscribed attitudes, the borrowing of Curnow's critical dictum about the time-life of a poem, the tinge of academicism in contemplating words as "an effective audible pattern," the claim for the poet and his "right to play building blocks with words." Meantime the core or matrix of all his poetry was a kind of sensuous passivity:

> Lying back in the chair to laugh or standing and smiling
> One would accept all fates, and even the gold
> Melancholy leaves of late autumn
> Would seem as natural as a child's toy.
>
> But labour and hunger strides the year
> In seasonal repetition, more harsh than tidal waters.
> The very rocks are cold: and they were lava once.
>
> So stand the dull green trees bearing the weather
> On solitary boughs; so the grey smoke of rain
> Drifts on a painted verge of sea and air,
> The fisherman casts his net to hold the tide.
> Chilly the light wind blowing. And dark the face of noon-day
> As at the inconsolable parting of friends.
>   (BWF, 29, "Sea Noon")

Blow, Wind of Fruitfulness, pervaded by a youthful romanticism, is preoccupied for three-quarters of its length with the idea of death and with man's Promethean struggle amid life's solitariness. Bleeding "on the cross of time," man endures the struggle, barred from that

>   perpetual day
> Where the bronze horses standing in a field

The Early Poetry

>   Lean on the wind and graze the hours away
>   Eden yet green for them and earth their shield.
>   (BWF, 16)

Somewhere beyond man glows the "unachieved Eden," while he is condemned to "our cold world that seems," the misty Niflheim of our present existence. Not that the stances are consistently held, or always clearly defined. Almost every poem deals with death and the grave, but there is more than one reference to "seasonal repetition" and the wind which both dissolves and creates. "I am man, child no longer / And I accept my death" (p. 14) he declares at one moment, and "*There is no death within.*" From the charnel-house tone a casual reader might gather that here is another poet more than "half in love with easeful death"; but Death is "no barren cycle," rather "A truth as eternal as life is eternal". Sometimes the two attitudes, wallowing in death or incorporating it into the meaning of one's life, seem fused: "Death is more deep than love: death is my spirit now." Death is confronted, and perhaps accepted, but only with a sense of deep loss. Man's mortal condition and his awareness of it — this is the primary sign and chief punishment of his fall from Eden, which is the cause of his sense of loss.

"Earth does at length her own sweet brood devour": recognition of this, the struggle to accept and assimilate it, is the chief ground of Baxter's early work. Part of the struggle is toward discovering why we exist if human existence leads but to death. Speaking of the poet's vocation in *Beyond the Palisade* he had said:

>   Could they break free
>   From the cave of day
>   Then would be nothing worth
>   But life, birth, death
>   And the wind-broken ground.

Later as we shall see, the cave will provide his protagonist's moment of initiation, but it is the dark cave, the cave of night, into which he must descend. In the present instance, presumably, the "cave of day" is Plato's cave, the images we encounter in our ordinary lives being mere illusion. Just as the night carries the double possibility, for Baxter, of being the ground of creation or destruction, so the day, used in many cases to refer to the perpetual light of Eden, has the other possibility of being the ground of illusion. That said, the lines quoted provide an important locus. Ultimately, for Baxter, the struggle is engaged and resolved on "the wind-broken ground" and involves (and here the ambiguities continue) "nothing of worth / But life, birth, death," the recurring pattern to which man is chained, and which is his glory.

Free of such ambiguity, the bronze horses live in "perpetual day," just as "The Antelopes" (p. 20) are "a race undying," and this prelapsarian state is shared by children. The poet prays "For One Going Overseas" (p. 27):

> Waken for her no war but resurrection
> (Lost the cold city and the mountain cloud)
> Of a child's anarchy, not lonely and not proud.

From about this time a Wordsworthian sense of the significance of the child-world enters his verse:

> I remember the roses of
> A childhood garden,
> And the first eyes of grief
> For flowers that redden
> Yet rot in garden mould.
>
> (p. 17)

This is the first, shocking discovery that the day is not perpetual, that in time, "when night falls," the "daylight children" "huddle close beside the unknown tall / Stone amphitheatre at the desert's rim" (p. 20). Night is death-knowledge, loss of unified vision (or banishment into Blake's "Single Vision," one-dimensional); night is yearning for instinctual unity, the "wild lost city of a mother's love," realization of our separateness.

In "Returned Soldier" (p. 22), one of the few poems of this period not I-centered, Baxter moves in the direction of social commentary, but the poem's chief concern is initiation into manhood, which is also submergence or loss of childhood. The tragedy of this initiation is the separateness it causes, from the green world of the garden, from one's fellow men. "Entitled now to call himself a man," shaped to it by an impoverished experience which yet will almost certainly be the major experience of his life, the boy no longer a boy goes

> Back to a city bed or station hut
> At maelstrom centre falling through the night
> To dreams where deeper than El Alamein

The Early Poetry

A buried childhood stirs with leaves and flowers
Remembered girls, the blurred and bitter waters.
Wakes to the midnight rafters and the rain.

The night image here corresponds in tone and direction to the opening lines of Edward Thomas' "Rain" (written when Thomas was soldiering in the First World War):

Rain, midnight rain, nothing but the wild rain
On this bleak hut, and solitude, and me
Remembering again that I shall die....[6]

Passive fatalism does not, however, quite capture the whole of *Blow, Wind of Fruitfulness*. "High Country Weather" (BWF, 15) is an intensely realised image of solitary but active stoicism, but it is an exhortation:

Alone we are born
And die alone;
Yet see the red-gold cirrus
Over snow-mountain shine.

Upon the upland road
Ride easy, stranger:
Surrender to the sky
Your heart of anger

while the wind, after all, is potentially fruitful and may have the power (in the language of the book's title-poem) to "Renew the single eye" (unified vision), since it blows "from the buried kingdom / Where heart and mind are one." Meanwhile the life endured is that of multiple vision, proliferation, chaos, of "The alley overgrown, no meaning now but loss: / Not that veritable garden where everything comes easy," the terrible dichotomy summoned up in "The Bay" (BWF, p. 37), one of the most passionately moving, and at the same time concrete, poems in the collection:

And by the bay itself were cliffs with carved names
And a hut on the shore beside the maori ovens.
We raced boats from the bank of the pumice creek
Or swam in those autumnal shallows
Growing cold in amber water, riding the logs
Upstream, and waiting for the taniwha.

> So now I remember the bay, and the little spiders
> On driftwood, so poisonous and quick.
> The carved cliffs and the great outcrying surf
> With currents round the rocks and the birds rising.
> A thousand times an hour is torn across
> And burned for the sake of going on living.
> But I remember the bay that never was
> And stand like stone, and cannot turn away.

J. E. Weir, in his useful discussion of *Blow, Wind of Fruitfulness*,[7] sees some of the later poems as implicitly affirmative, but does not note that the book as a whole is rather oddly organized. "Envoi" (p. 39), placed at the three-quarter point, written somewhat in the tone of Eliot's *Poems 1920*, is a dejected and even suicidal poem bemoaning life as a university student, which has caused to be *"Lost, one original heart and mind."* This poem (an early Baxter comment on education, a subject which was later to engage his attention a great deal) is then followed by nine others more positive and concrete than those preceding them.

First of these, "Elegy for my Father's Father" (BWF, p. 40) is to the refrain: "He knew in the hour he died / That his heart had never spoken," but rejoices in the grandfather's manly skills and the sober "burning-glass of his mind," and celebrates in rhythms with a new, sinewy confidence that, finally, "his heart was unafraid." Following this the "Letter to Noel Ginn, II" has an unaccustomed satirical bite and a foursquare sense of the realities of existence:

> So poets learn to live like other men
> For money, lovers, or the friends with whom
> Music can animate a sunless room
> And rouse the rumour of a different Sun
> That shines the same though endless night draw on
> And wakes the dead heart from its numbered tomb.

Three of the remaining poems, "Let Time Be Still," "The Track," and "Tunnel Beach" deal in some measure with the possibility of affirmation through human sexuality. "Let Time Be Still" (p. 45), least concrete of the three, is a lyrical celebration of the sexual act as return to Eden ("the timelost season / Of perpetual summer"), "The Track" (p. 47), more particularized and perhaps consequently more equivocal in its attitudes, evokes the tenderness of sexual encounter but sets it in uncertain, storm-threatening weather. Storm threatens

The Early Poetry

still in "Tunnel Beach" (p. 48), the most powerful of the three poems. In spite of its declaration that

> The honey of your moving thighs
> Drew down the cirrus sky, your doves about the beach
> Shut out sea thunder with their wings and stilled the lonely air

it is dominated by sea's thunder and rolling waves. The lovers come in sight "Of the first garden," but the sighting is momentary only. Emergence from the tunnel this time is not to the dazzle of daylight but to "the loud / Voice of the sea's women riding / All storm to come," which storm may be said to include the inevitable waves of the sex drive. Hovering in the background of the poem is the traditional double-image of woman, as witch ("the witch tormented wood") and Virgin-Mother ("No virgin mother bore / My heart wave eaten"). We shall look at this in greater detail later, in dealing with the whole subject of human love in Baxter's work. Here, in summary, the "doves" of the girl in the poem do not make up for the lack of the single dove, which is not born of "the womb of cloud." In all three poems, then, affirmation is intense, but merely transient.

Another poem, "Haast Pass" (p. 46) rejects the static life, the life of mere nature, which is time-rooted and can teach us nothing of how to live our human lives. Rather than merely become one with the "seasonal repetition" of plants and stones, the protagonist adjures himself to "Return from here" for

> This earth was never ours. Remember
> Rather the tired faces in the pub
> The children who have never grown. Return
> To the near death, the loves like garden flowers.

Rather than accept as one's portion the unencumbered cycle of nature, one should engage in the responsibilities of his human lot, including those which involve him in the acceptance of mortality and his own part in the cycle of seasonal repetition. This is an account of coming back to life from the temptation of potential living death.

But the triumphant expression of this return is "The Cave" (p. 49):

> In a hollow of the fields, where one would least expect it,
> Stark and suddenly this limestone buttress:

A tree whose roots are bound about the stones,
Broad-leaved, hides well that crevice in the base
That leads, one guesses, to the sunless kingdom
Where souls endure the ache of Proserpine.

Entering where no man it seemed
Had come before, I found a rivulet
Beyond the rock door running in the dark,
Where it sprang from in the heart of the hill
No one could tell: alone
It ran like Time there in the dank silence.

I spoke once and my voice resounded
Among the many pillars. Further in
Were bones of sheep that strayed and died
In nether darkness, brown and water-worn.
The smell of earth was like a secret language
That dead men speak and we have long forgotten.

The whole weight of the hill hung over me;
Gladly I would have stayed there and been hidden
From every beast that moves beneath the sun,
From age's enmity and love's contagion:
But turned and climbed back to the barrier
Pressed through and came to dazzling daylight out.

Susceptible to Freudian interpretation (and not inappropriately, since Baxter was acutely conscious of "The Freudian fog-belt"), especially since it follows immediately two poems concerned with sexual awakening, the poem's deeper concern is with the dark world at the roots of the tree of life, the inextricable connection between life and death. For the cave is the house of Hades, realm of Pluto and Proserpine. Rock door and rivulet are counterparts of the White Rock and dreaded rivers of the Underworld. Significantly, Pluto is not mentioned, whereas "the ache of Proserpine" refers to her suffering aspect and not her cruelty in goading the Furies. This locates the poem's center. In darkness Proserpine is the hard, unyielding mistress of Hades (we may here equate her with the witch, the Terrible Mother in her negative phase), but when she is goddess of spring she revisits the earth bearing a cornucopia overflowing with flowers. Thus the return is reemergence from darkness, a rebirth from the womb of death. Vincent O'Sullivan suggests another dimension:

The Early Poetry

In the light of Baxter's own remarks of the origins of a poem, "The Cave" may also be read as the inception and birth of poetry itself, the reassembly of scattered or even uncomfortable elements in life into something new and healthy. The imagery is not inappropriate for the pressure of the mind working deliberately as well as unconsciously upon these elements, and through distress, the emergence to the new voice of that last line — so close to Valéry's line in "Narcisse", "Que tu brilles enfin, terme pour de ma course!"[8]

This interpretation may be placed alongside Baxter's own description of an experience he had when he was seven years old: "I climbed up to a hole in a bank in a hill above the sea, and there fell into the attitude of *listening* out of which poems may rise — not to the sound of the sea, but to the unheard sound of which poems are translations — it was then that I first endured that intense effort of *listening*, like a man chained to the ground trying to stand upright and walk" (MH, 124). Since he has told us also that he wrote his first poem when he was seven, this is like an account of a birth, or rebirth. Far, then, from being as Weir suggests "a retreat from a reality which had become too hard to handle" (Weir, 26) — even though lines 20 - 22 may support such a reading — "The Cave" realizes the moment of second birth, when "daylight" has been recovered after descent into "the sunless kingdom." Having gone into the dark, the protagonist reemerges with a true sense of the light.[9]

This reading seems to be extended in the positive, Christian statement of the ensuing "Morning and Evening Calm":

> the Lord has spoken
> from no devouring whirlwind, but the still
> green garden of a world-sustaining Will.
> O tenderly by him the heart is broken. . . .
> (p. 50)

Equally, "O Wind Blowing" (BWF, 11) now seems to be in some kind of structural relationship with "The Cave," for the wind as natural element is akin to Proserpine, bringing dissolution and creation (carrying away the dead leaves, carrying the seed). Lying close to the earth, whose smell in the cave is "like a secret language / that dead men speak": "Under the sodden pines I have lain and listened / To the voice of quiet death speaking from air and branches." But having listened, having discovered death: "I looked to my feet and among the rotted needles / Saw hyacinths bloom." Again this is a poem of the cycle, of rebirth, of the young Hyacinthus slain by Apollo's arrow, commemorated in Apollo's grief by a beautiful flower, so that each spring "Frail Hyacinthus rises from green earth." The poet has discovered the "truth as eternal as life is eternal," crucial to all his work thenceforth:

> No barren cycle is this
> No grave of stars forever more lifeless
> Rather a truth, living, incomprehensible
> Clear with the clearness and opaqueness of water.

The foregoing interpretation of "The Cave" may suggest why the book concludes with the untypical "Farmhand" (p. 51), a portrait corresponding to "Returned Soldier," but different in quality, more meditative, less mechanical. The farmhand's reticence, his limitations, his slowness and solitariness, are movingly evoked, and there is life in him, "awkward hopes" and "envious dreams." Unlike the returned soldier, he is not pictured passively, lying awake alone at midnight, but forking stooks in harvesttime, effortlessly strong and accomplished in pursuing his life's natural calling. Thus the collection is rounded out on a life-affirming note, the detailed and sympathetic delineation of an individual man.

Blow, Wind of Fruitfulness is, at its center, the locating and clarifying of a personal quest of the soul and, equally, it continues Baxter's discovery of his own voice as poet. Reviewing the book in *Landfall*, Allen Curnow traces the influence of Baxter's New Zealand forerunners, R. A. K. Mason and A. R. D. Fairburn, and of M. H. Holcroft's "meditation upon mountain and rain forest."[10] As Curnow saw it, the older poets had turned away from "assertions about New Zealand" in favor of more personal and universal themes. He concludes: "The way in which certain conceptions of his country haunt the background of Mr. Baxter's poetry, having receded from the positive foreground of older poets, encourages the belief that something of continuing effect was achieved by them." For a "tradition" of good poetry not more than a quarter of a century old, this was an important consideration! Baxter more than bore out the implied hope that he would continue to build and strengthen the national poetry. In later years he was to take an antichauvinist position in literary quarrels about New Zealand, but ultimately he was to

The Early Poetry

prove much ampler, as a poet and individual, than both parties to the argument.

III The Night Shift

Between the publication of his first two major books Baxter wrote the group of poems published much later as one section of *The Night Shift* (1957),[11] a joint work containing "poems on aspects of love" by Baxter, Charles Doyle, Louis Johnson, and Kendrick Smithyman. In relation both to its handling of the theme, and the individual contributions, the book was not a success. Baxter's section, "Songs of the Desert," was described not unfairly by Erik Schwimmer as "a series of loudly intoned approximations,"[12] and it does exhibit Baxter's dangerous facility in employing the stock responses of decadent romanticism. Yet, inevitably, even these poems (and it has been said that Baxter's are the weakest in the book) have their moments of powerful perception, perhaps strongest in his concluding poem, one of the few references in his work to his earliest sexual experience:

> Out of the past I summon Pyrrha,
> Girl of plaited wheat, first
> Mentor of love revealed in dying.
> She has come back with a burning-glass
> To whom once my thoughts clung
> Like branches under weirs tumbling. . . .
> (p. 22)

A more coherent, if derivative, treatment of the theme of erotic love and its suburban consequences is "Cressida," a lyric sequence published in *Landfall* in 1951. Under the formal influence of Auden and Yeats, the sixteen-part series recounts Cressida's unfaithfulness to her absent lover and her consequent seduction. Predictably, she becomes pregnant and, in observance of puritan morality, is forced to marry the "wrong man." She, as child and virgin, had dreamed of "a snakeless garden," a hope which is betrayed. Nor, since he is human, can she expect that her first, "true" lover will "Forgive as one did in Gethsemane's garden." Thus, in despair, she addresses her unborn child:

> But you, stranger in my body's house
> Sheltered, dreaming your deepwater dream,

> Who make my shape strange in a looking-glass:
> You, curled in the dusk of the first garden,
> Forgive me if I call your weight a winter,
> Castaway, to an older sun constant.[13]

Again the reader encounters the images of the garden, the ambiguities of the virgin and the whore, and the "older sun" — these are to prove rich categories of Baxter's inner world.

IV Poems Unpleasant

The first phase of Baxter's career may be seen as culminating in the publication of *Poems Unpleasant* (1952),[14] another joint book, this time with Louis Johnson and Anton Vogt. Closely associated in the 1950s and early 1960s, Baxter and Johnson were for a time students at Wellington Teachers College, where Vogt was an imaginative and influential lecturer (described by Baxter in *Recent Trends* as "himself a commendable poet.") Among Vogt's students of that period were other significant New Zealand writers, such as Alistair Campbell, Noel Hilliard, and Barry Mitcalfe, and his work included fostering the lively publications of the Glenco Press; but the association with Baxter and Johnson is perhaps the chief fruit of the period.

Poems Unpleasant is a contrast in styles. Vogt's social commentary has a characteristic light witty touch, though sometimes contrived; Johnson is much heavier in line, more vocative in mood. What Baxter shares with Johnson, here and elsewhere, is a faculty for seeing experience in mythological terms, for perceiving the archetype behind the commonplace. By comparison, Vogt is adroit at literary allusion, and is a sharp observer of behaviors and surfaces.

Baxter's poems, still, are haunted by literary echoes ("A rough wind shakes the barren boughs of custom"), and he is much preoccupied by, and skillful with, traditional literary forms. More clearly now he perceives the terrifying split between deadening habit and the forgotten "language of the heart"; he views pessimistically the fate of "wormsmeat, man" in "this blind century" and especially on the "castrate island" (New Zealand) where "the tiger walks with wounded paw" and "Anthropoid Adam mourns his lost estate." Here again is the lament for the creative energy of the lost, whole, animistic vision.

Several poems, "Never No More," "Conversation in a Road," "The Surfman's Story," and "Mill Girl" explore the destructive

The Early Poetry

effects of custom on the creative force of sexuality, of how in our society sexual discovery leads to "a hamstrung heart and no way back" (the fate of Baxter's Cressida) or to hypocrisy and superficiality. Having made a suicide pact with her lover, the girl in "The Surfman's Story" (p. 14) eventually and happily marries her rescuer, thus demonstrating the superficiality of erotic romantic vows. "Mill Girl" (p. 19) explores the gap between romantic pretensions and social realities. Waiting "in the ignorant garden of her wishes" for Mr. Right," the girl succumbs, and:

> On wet park leaves, or on a mattress in a back
> Room at the party, loses what none can keep —
> Rough and ready, before the keg runs dry
> Fumbled and forced — yet willing, ready to learn the knack.

Richest of Baxter's selection is its concluding poem, "The Homecoming" (p. 21):

> Odysseus has come home, to the gully farm
> Where the macrocarpa windbreak shields a house
> Heavy with time's reliques — the brown-filmed photographs
> Of ghosts more real than he; the mankind-measuring arm
> Of a pendulum clock; and true yet to her vows,
> His mother, grief's Penelope. At the blind the sea wind laughs.
>
> The siege more long and terrible than Troy's
> Begins again. A Love demanding all,
> Hypochondriacal, seadark and contentless;
> This was the sour ground that nurtured a boy's
> Dream of freedom; this, in Circe's hall
> Drugged him; his homecoming finds this, more relentless.
>
> She does not say, 'You have changed'; nor could she
>   imagine any
> Otherwise to the quiet maelstrom spinning
> In the circle of their days. Still she would wish to
>   carry
> Him folded within her, shut from the wild and many
> Voices of life's combat, in the cage of beginning;
> She counts it natural that he should never marry.
>
> She will cook his meals; complain of the south weather
> That wrings her joints. And he — rebels; and yields

> To the old covenant — calms the bleating
> Ewe in birth travail. The smell of saddle leather
> His sacrament; or the sale day drink; yet hears beyond
>   sparse fields
> On reef and cave the sea's hexameter beating.

This is rooted in New Zealand ways, the old covenant of farm life, for the protagonist, "The smell of saddle leather / His sacrament; or the sale day drink"; but interestingly the Penelope-figure is mother rather than wife, and as a representative of Penelope's patient faithfulness she is a figure of profound irony. Loved, she is yet the Spiderwitch (of "The Dark Side," another poem in the selection), opposite to the child-woman who is the Muse of cloudy visions and of "earthly paradise that the human race cannot enter" (MH, 65). Baxter's own comment on one of his later poems: "Henley Pub," illuminates "The Homecoming": "My hero is a man who has not travelled far from the gates of the womb; hence his extreme vulnerability to the faults of the flesh. There is an undeveloped Oedipal quality in his relation to his mistress, in his closeness to water and earth, in the complete passivity, of his Marian devotion. Women are all mothers to him . . ."(MH, 75). From such homecomings the poet has much further yet to travel, and the arc of his career is a movement from passivity to action, from·acquiescence to rebellion.

Baxter was not an intellectually complex poet, but his vision of human experience goes far beyond the merely intellectual, and this is apparent even in his early work. His vision encompasses the child born to darkness, whose fall from innocence is his awakening to death. Without this awareness the child would dwell in the earthly paradise, but it is in his death-discovery that he becomes a man. By definition, man is his own destroyer. In life he can attain a temporary contact with Eden through following his sexual instinct. Through it he creates, but he does so in the knowledge that whatever is created by man must die. However, any one human death is not final and life itself is, in some sense, eternal. With this sense of the eternal, Baxter set out on his later journey, toward eventual fruitfulness.

CHAPTER 3

The Door Ajar to Let the Furies Enter

DELIBERATELY in this chapter I shall relinquish some measure of critical distance. Central to my subject is the special flavor of Wellington in the 1950s — a small, grubby, cramped precipitous town locked in by high hills and set in a magnificent harbor. Baxter, a stocky man of five-foot-seven or so, with a large head, used to scuttle about the rabbit warren streets as if in flight from some unseen pursuer.

Belatedly after the young prodigy, his own generation set about establishing itself — such poets as Alistair Campbell, Louis Johnson, and, in the large commercial metropolis to the north, Kendrick Smithyman. At first mutedly, a battle of generations had begun, which became a literary guerrilla war between nationalists and "internationalists," and which continued sputtering until the mid-1960s.[1] If Curnow felt in 1948 that he could categorically claim Baxter as a poet of the New Zealand experience, happily following a path fresh-trodden by the pioneers of the 1930s, Robert Chapman could say within a few years, "being a New Zealander is for him a matter of biography and not aesthetic vocation."[2] Curnow's critical writings show that one of his main concerns is to anatomize the distinctive native qualities of his poets' work, whereas Chapman in his Oxford anthology preface declared that the New Zealander shared the common experience of all Westerners.[3] That Baxter was overwhelmingly of the latter persuasion is evident from his prose comments alone published in the numbers of *New Zealand Poetry Yearbook* and *Salient Literary Issue* from 1953 to 1955.

I The Fallen House

Having saluted the young Baxter's technical virtuosity, Chapman locates the emotional center of the strongest poems in *The Fallen House* as "a conviction of loss — loss of hope, order and delight"

(211). Although then heavily conscious of poetry as an aesthetic performance, Baxter more and more emerged as one who would speak with the fallen, his fellows: "Mr Baxter's doctrine goes roughly thus. The highest value is to be attached to the free flow of the emotions and what confines that freedom in daily living deserves to be denounced. He wants us 'to know an age where all our lives have scope'. His own childhood he sees in this book as an idyllic 'waking dream' where this full flow of feeling occurred without consciousness of itself, a pre-serpent Eden from which "time" expelled him" (211).

Meantime, about the "expelled" Baxter gathered stories of days and weeks of drunken progresses, of how he (the mailman) collapsed in a public lavatory leaving undelivered letters scattered among the stench, or fell into a boozy sleep in the very post office, or tossed his full mailbag under a gorse bush. Amid his frequent repairings to the Grand Hotel, with Anton Vogt, Brian Bell, and others, his preoccupation with childhood's lost innocence deepened:

> From this black swamp where I have lain among
> Serpents, or chained to the Caucasian rock
> Heard wingbeat of those vultures that attend
> The dying and tear soft flesh with brazen talons —
>
> I recall another morning and another sun
> Myself a child high in the milk-cart riding,
> Odour of fresh dung at the horse's heels
> And calm daybreak upon the sea horizon.
>
> (FH, 10)

Fallen, he is haunted by a dream of time defeated, of "Childhood and age in one green cradle joined" (FH, 21). The "relationship of Time and childhood," says Kendrick Smithyman in *A Way of Saying*, is a central theme in New Zealand poetry.[4] Certainly, before Baxter, Allen Curnow had explored it, perceiving human experience, for example, in his "Children, Swimmers"[5] as "Your flesh against time's fathoms." Ambiguously, Curnow speaks of how the flesh "astonishes with a breath this drowned/ Valley where tides are lost and love's dead found." Baxter never fully accepts such an Atlantean view, nor does he retreat to mild ironies regarding New Zealand education, which Curnow does in his later piece, "Not in Narrow Seas."[6]

Through his emergence from the cave, Baxter's protagonist

The Door Ajar to Let the Furies Enter

knows despair, profoundly, because in flashes of vision he has discerned its opposite, completeness; but he cannot at will retrieve the vision, so he searches for the way back toward it, seeking "Leisure to stroll and see Him unafraid / Who walked with Adam once in the green shade" (FH, 16, "For My Father"). "Time slew the first Adam/ In me" he tells us in "Temple Basin" (FH, 18), and the book is haunted by glimpses of the "veritable garden." Aware of "the numberless drowned" (the dead) the poet at Virginia Lake invokes "the garden and the talking water / Where once a child walked and wondered." He longs for it:

> O out of this rock tomb
> Of labyrinthine grief, I start and cry
> Toward his real day: The undestroyed
> Fantastic Eden of a waking dream.
> (FH, 19)

Carried into the poetry reading, upright though drunk, his feet barely touching the ground as he is supported under the crook of each arm by a fellow poet, Baxter will somehow give a fine memorable reading in that sonorous, cultivated voice of his, lingering meditatively over the syllables. By fits and starts gregarious enough, he yet had the ambience of a solitary, introverted figure. Both moments of melancholy knowledge and glimpses of Eden tend, in *The Fallen House*, to be associated with solitary creatures, as in "The Hermit," "Prospector," "Song for an Old Soak," "The Doll," "Venetian Blinds," and "A Rented Room." Speaking in 1954 on "Symbolism in New Zealand Poetry" Baxter suggested that the dominant symbol is "man alone." His earliest book review had been of Mulgan's *Man Alone* and Baxter was aware that such a figure is common in modern literature. He felt nonetheless that "in New Zealand prose and verse it has taken on a local colour and a central importance" (FA, 70). The "man alone" tends to be on the fringe of society, isolated from every social aim, eccentric. For Baxter, by definition the artist is such a man, because he has kept some of the attributes of the child and, clinging to his own fantasy life, "retains the early image of himself as important — capable of learning the secret of the universe" (FA, 70).

Like a child he has "a love of the world, and a wish that it should expand to his love." "Venetian Blinds" (FH, 30), one of the many poems set in a solitary room, portrays the child's gradual loss of fantasy, laying bare the terrible contrasts of the real world's "zebra light" (prison bars of multiplicity), until, as he grows older "His daydream paths converged till one path led / Him out of childhood trembling and afraid / Toward a dream of Woman . . ." (FH, 30), who is the occasion of his fall into "average light, no mystery." A hallucinatory quality is present in many of these poems, and notice in both quotations above the mesmeric use of "toward." From this same period a somewhat overstrained group of "Prose Poems" contrasts Woman with the often sought-after "crony and jail companion," implying that all women derive from the Furies[7] (see chapter 7 below) and hinting perhaps at a characteristically Antipodean secret yearning, for mateship rather than heterosexuality-leading-to-domesticity.

Again alone in a room he — at nineteen, initiate — is momentarily deluded into sensing himself "at the good centre," but he is "the green boy come of age — / Not seeing the handsized cloud in the clear sky / And the door ajar to let the Furies enter" (FH, 31). Baxter's focus for the book, the fallen *house*, was brilliantly intuitive, as a reading of chapter 1 of Gaston Bachelard's *The Poetics of Space* will show. Bachelard says: "For our house is our corner of the world . . . our first universe. . . . " And, "In the life of a man, the house thrusts aside contingencies, its councils of continuity are unceasing. Without it, man would be a dispersed being."[8] Throughout *The Fallen House* poem after poem suggests fear of the outside world. For the protagonist entering the world (and the world entering him) becomes more deeply alone. (In Baxter, as there often is in such cases, the counter-element, the Rilkean awareness of "I spoke almost to no one; for it was my joy to be alone," is present, but the sense of isolation is dominant.) In his guise as an "old soak" (drunkard), whom life has drawn out and yet also bypassed, he longs to return to beginnings: "I seek the green inn/ Where life and death begin" (FH, 25) (which hints both the green garden and the first hospice — yet, of course, there was "No room at the inn"!).

Some seek to rediscover Eden garden on this earth, as did the prospector (FH, 33) who went off and built his stone shack by himself (as Bachelard calls it, "the simplest of human plants"), to live by panning for gold in the rough Kawarau River, establishing "A garden at the back/ Cool with mint and parsley," only to be defeated by time:

> Till they came at length and took him
> To die in a city house
> Alone as he never was.

Meanwhile the green briar invades his stone hut:

> Hut and matted garden
> Stand yet, the bare emblem
> Of some great love forgotten . . .
> (FH, 34)

Thus is life in time, but it is part of a cycle. The protagonist in "The Hermit" (FH, 27) had in his earlier days been a husband and father. Left now a "worn-out soak" and odd-job man, with failing faculties, he nonetheless reads his Bible and smiles in recollection of the past: "and soon a wave will take him, or the cold/ March gales, his lean flesh a sodden mound,/ His spent soul to that river where none grow old." (FH, 28).

To interpret like this, seeking a pervasive motif in the fabric, is perhaps to neglect evaluation. Neither "Prospector" nor "The Hermit" is among the better poems in *The Fallen House*, and for all its exegetical usefulness the conclusion of "The Hermit" has an inescapable air of sentimentality. Many years later, Baxter opens *Jerusalem Daybook* (1971) with a brief account of two dreams. In the first he appears as ship's engineer; the second concerns a hermit walking a bare path beside a church. "It is the barest place in the world. A sense of endless grief and waiting permeates the dream. . . . The path leads into an absolute solitude. . . . Between the engine room and the solitary path, my life uncoils like a rope let free from a lifesaver's drum. That's the way one lives. I live among *nga mokai*. But I think I may die without company. All our fables blow away like *smoke* before we come to God" (JD, 7). Juxtaposed, the passage tells much about the great inward distance Baxter had traveled in twenty years.

More limited in its claims, "The Doll" (FH, 39) approaches the same theme of the old man near death, whose garden orchard once he is dead becomes "Now ruinous with bramble, overhung/ By tattered bluegum." Alive, remembering the "tale of Samson's youth" wherein the dead lion's bones "brought honey forth," "knife in hand"

> he carved a wooden doll
> (By what fond myth, ancestral memory stirred?)
> Hammered an iron band about its skull
> And set it firm on a post outside his yard
> Visible sign of mana, keeping guard
> On haycock, barn and byre, with new life kindled
> While his life like the old moon daily dwindled.

Such ritual (expressing "traditional piety," but also perhaps devotion to art) is already for Baxter, searching, too little to live by, not substantial enough to shore up "the mansion, ruinous, of the human heart." God is there, or the possibility of Him, but distant, and for man perhaps too much a "blinding glass," manifest in the wild grandeur of nature:

> Sky's purity, the altar cloth of snow
> On deathly summits laid; or avalanche
> That shakes the rough moraine with giant laughter;
> Snowplume and whirlwind — what are these
> But His flawed mirror, who gave the mountain strength
> And dwells in holy calm, undying freshness?
>
> Therefore we turn, hiding our souls' dullness
> From that too blinding glass; turn to the gentle
> Dark of our human daydream, child and wife,
> Patience of stone and soil, the lawful city
> Where man may live, and no wild trespass
> Of what's eternal shake his grave of time.
>
> (FH, 36)

(We are conscious here perhaps of too great a degree of merely "traditional piety." Are the "holy calm, undying freshness" much more than figments?) A brand of stoic fatalism seems evident. Turning to the "patience of stone and soil," the protagonist apparently feels the world is a place governed by fate:

> Four of them rode the warm ancestral air
> But one flew straight to the flax bush shade
> And slid down heavy on a forked blade
> And caught by the neck and hung and strangled there.
>
> (FH, 11)

Part of that fate is the strange perversity of man's nature, already revealed in the child as he moves from his daylight self, and turns to

The Door Ajar to Let the Furies Enter

the dark. A gang of boys, in the parable poem "Wild Bees," "masked to the eyes like plundering desperadoes" and "waiting for light to drain from the wounded sky," came and smoked out the bees:

> Fallen then the city of instinctive wisdom.
> Tragedy is written distinct and small:
> A hive burned on a cool night in summer.
> But loss is a precious stone to me, a nectar
> Distilled in time, preaching the truth of winter
> To the fallen heart that does not cease to fall.
> (FH, 24)

Together with Baxter's sense of a childhood Eden and the Just City he declares for in *Recent Trends*, "the city of instinctive wisdom" is part of the true order of things. Fate may govern fallen man's world, but his situation is not totally determined. Guilty of Original Sin he may be, but he can look back to what has been lost — "the promise of prodigious noon," the abandoned garden — and the loss itself may be cherished. Man, too, has his instinctive wisdom, in the form of a latent energy which Baxter commonly associates in these early days with the lion, but which later (particularly in his associative nexus "the lion's den") he consistently treats more negatively. Now he contrasts the world of the "genteel elders" who sit "On straight-backed parlour chairs," with the child's vision seen through a glass door (FH, 44), a vision beyond talk of consequences, of "a burning lion" and "green, yellow, red/ Men like angels," a growth-hallucination, a vision actually in himself, "mirror/of your heart's falcon eye," grasped in a moment experienced by one "as if not born to die," but to discover:

> The green lane that leads to the wishing well
> The secret house the fertile wilderness
> Where grief and memory are reconciled.
> Angels of fire and ice guard well that garden.
> (FH, 20 - 21)

Yet the central image of this selection is the dwelling fallen into ruin: the hive, "city of instinctive wisdom," destroyed, the "rotten boards" of the hermit's shack, the prospector's hut conquered by briar, the very heart's "mansion" ruinous, and, rounding out the book, the visit to Duffy's Farm, where:

> Ungainly
> The sprawled stones fireblackened could
> Recall man; though where the house stood
> Stands ragged thistle only.

Time is victor over the lost, shared "beaten light fondly flaring." As for the humans, former inhabitants of Duffy's Farm: "Pale now and gossamer-thin/ The web their lives had woven" (FH, 48).

II Traveller's Litany

Among many beautiful passages of *The Notebooks of Malte Laurids Brigge*, Rilke has one virtuoso piece on the necessary link between poetry and experience (dare one invoke it again, "the reality prior to the poem"!): "For verses are not, as people imagine, simply feelings (those one has early enough), — they are experiences. For the sake of a single verse, one must see many cities, men and things, one must know the animals, one must feel how the birds fly and know the gesture with which the little flowers open in the morning. One must be able to think back to roads...."[9] Poem after poem in *The Fallen House* shows advance on his earlier work, chiefly by increase of what Baxter himself later referred to as "experiential knowledge" which he thought the very basis of poetry. With a few lapses, they are based on detailed recording of concrete experiences. Since Baxter is primarily a maker of parables and perceiver of myths this adherence to the concrete is vitally necessary. He is not a poet of ideas, but of mythologized events, or, as Bachelard might have said, "a phenomenologist of the soul." His parable-making and mythologizing methods imply teaching and imply archetypes behind incidents. Concreteness, therefore, is of the essence. Strange and disappointing then that his next work, *Traveller's Litany* (1955), should fall into the twin snares of pastiche and generalization; all the more strange because he had, in the interim, spoken cogently on modern poetry in his MacMillan Brown lectures, published that same year as *The Fire and the Anvil*. Meantime the periodicals had netted some of his best poems, such as "Seraphion" and "Elegy at the Year's End."

Traveller's Litany expresses Baxter's Marian devotion ("Marial," Owen Leeming calls it, I notice). In what might well have been a major statement he contrasts Eros (combined with Thanatos by "the bitter stars") and Mary, Mother, "thou who dost bruise under thy heel the serpent"; but the sequence rises to no necessary order and, redolent of literary echoes as it is, makes uncomfortable reading as a devotional act. What it does is to bring into somewhat muzzy focus Baxter's sense of the split nature of woman. At the same time he was becoming progressively more conscious of man's split nature. In "Notes Towards an Aesthetic" he sees the split as between Orpheus and Promethus, figure of song and figure of power:

> When Prometheus asks the meaning of Orpheus' song, Orpheus replies — "Listen again"
> "But", says Prometheus, "does it incite men to the practice of virtue?"
> "No, it restores to them the freedom to do good and evil"[10]

"Freedom to do good and evil" worked in Baxter's psyche in those years to make both him and his work appear extremely erratic; but beneath this had begun, it now seems, the slow awakening of an interior harmony.

III Numbers

The mid-1950s witnessed an increase in Baxter's all-round writing activities. He wrote a considerable amount of speculative prose and short fiction; his first play *Jack Winter's Dream*, was written, published, and performed (see chapter 9 below), and he even offered us the clever parodies of *The Iron Breadboard* (1957). This period witnessed the emergence of the Wellington periodical *Numbers*, and the group around it. Ten issues were published between 1954 and 1959; and, erratic, irregular, and unkempt as it was, the magazine became a rallying point. Some of the older poets had already become disenchanted with Johnson's editing of the *New Zealand Poetry Yearbook*, and there were many signs of the rift between generations and nationalists-internationalists. The influential and respected essayist M. H. Holcroft devoted an editorial in *The New Zealand Listener* to the subject of "Lisping in Numbers." Even the Communist weekly *The People's Voice* ran a piece late in 1954 headed "Literary Decadence in New Magazine," which trumpeted that "the poets hitch their wagons to such waning stars as the madman Alasteir Crowley and the fatuous 'e.e. cummings.' . . . The prose is limp. There is the faint stale odour of Henry Miller. . . ." But, withal, the magazine was highly relevant to Baxter's life as a writer. Wellington, after all New Zealand's capital city, became a lively center of writing only about 1949 (Glover, Curnow, and the Caxton Press had seen to it that most such activity was centered on Christchurch from the late 1930s on). With the short-lived magazines *Hilltop* and *Arachne* (both perhaps more judicious and conservative than *Numbers*) emerged the talents of a variety of figures, the poets among them being Alistair Campbell, Pat Wilson, Hubert Witheford, and W. H. Oliver (with Louis Johnson coming to the scene independently). First Baxter and then Glover arrived ready to add distinctive talents. Another poet, Anton Vogt, with a group of students at the Teachers' College (soon attended by Campbell, Baxter, Barry Mitcalfe, Johnson, and, somewhat later, by Noel Hilliard) founded the Glenco Press, for a year or two a producer of bouncy small publications.

When a number of its mentors left New Zealand (some to study overseas and return, others to leave for good) the promising *Arachne* became defunct. Its successor was *Numbers*, which from the start reflected the situation of its editors. Of the five people who originated the magazine, two dropped out of the scheme almost immediately. The remaining three, who carried *Numbers* for most of its ten issues, were Baxter, Johnson, and Charles Doyle, all primarily poets. Erik Schwimmer (later editor of the Maori journal *Te Ao Hou*) was an influence behind the scenes. Because Doyle was inexperienced and Baxter elusive, even "fugitive," *Numbers* was sustained by Louis Johnson, who did nearly all the editorial digging and took care of the slender finances involved. Both *Numbers* and the *New Zealand Poetry Yearbook* are stamped with Johnson's limitations and virtues: willingness to explore, to run risks, and to attack social attitudes which seemed repressive or just plain senseless; sensitivity, but also a slapdash style of presentation and a somewhat careless openness to work of extremely variable quality, often dealt with over a beer at the Royal Oak Hotel or in the offices of a printer for whom Johnson then worked. Already he found the Curnow-Brasch "establishment" hidebound, guilty of an inward-looking nationalism which put a premium upon pseudo-Georgian verse. He, in contrast, gathered the litterateurs for parties at his pleasantly rambling Epuni house, at one time almost entirely decorated in black and white (hard enamel paint, black and white fabrics, model knights in black, white, and, a necessary compromise, silver), where Baxter recited from beery memory (and beautifully at that) whole stretches of Dylan Thomas' *Death and Entrances*, his copy of which he kept permanently in the right-hand pocket of his shabby sports coat.

The Door Ajar to Let the Furies Enter

Numbers was much less cool in tone than the more solidly established *Landfall*. In early issues the idea of dadaism was invoked, but *Numbers* never came within reach of dada, though Johnson had a stab at it, and the invocation probably reflects his desire to be part of an international "scene" and also the group's instinctive urge (helped on by such matters as the Holcroft editorial) to *épater le bourgeois*. Both Johnson and Baxter had considerable creative energy, but each was disadvantaged by the thinness of the culture in which he had to subsist. Neither could be blamed for the circumstance that, in those years at least, not enough good writing was available in New Zealand to sustain at a high standard even two literary magazines, though the very situation makes monopoly undesirable. In the event *Numbers* never became fully integrated (even when near the end of its career it took on Schwimmer and Peter Bland, both energetic and lively minds, as additional editors); nor did it ever become fully aware of its own purposes. Among a good deal of amateurish, dull work it published a few fine things (by Baxter, Maurice Duggan, J. C. Sturm, among others). Feebly enough, I suppose, it yet gave life to the possibility of an alternative to the official culture. Its pages, so uncertain in quality, containing unpredictable bright flashes, are as good a reflection as any of Baxter's life at this time: his alcoholism (which he often spoke and wrote about himself) and involvement with Alcoholics Anonymous; his continuing and deepening engagement with Christianity; his growing disenchantment with laboring as an editor in the educational bureaucracy. At about this time the "street life" of the New Zealand cities, hitherto barren, with pubs and milk bars (both commonly seedy) as the only refuges, was enriched by the introduction of "espresso bars," coffeelounges which were furnished in a manner unaccustomedly splendiferous (actually it was bourgeois chi-chi, mostly vinyl and chrome). Baxter was a great frequenter of such places, partially because they provided chess sets and he was a fine chess player. A brief passage of my book *Earth Meditations* speaks of

> deep
> night memories — the Picasso
> Coffee Bar —
> flukily
> taking Jim Baxter
> with a fool's mate . . .

I do not mention that he then proceeded to thrash me, one game after another, for six games, hunched over the table like a gnome, fully concentrated. Baxter was like that, capable of extraordinary lapses of attention, of purveying quantities of absentminded potboiling verse, but at his most intense he produced work of a rare incandescence, and a fair measure of it comes from that period.

IV In Fires of No Return

That chess game occurred in 1958, the year Baxter spent time with the Trappists in Hawke's Bay, the year he went to India, and the year he received his first overseas "recognition," with the publication by Oxford University Press in London of *In Fires of No Return*. This book and its Oxford successor, *Howrah Bridge and Other Poems* (1961), are puzzles in chronology. For his new audience Baxter naturally culled from what he considered the best of his already-published work. Of the three sections of *In Fires of No Return*, all of section 1 had appeared in his three Caxton Press collections; section 2 is work from *Poems Unpleasant* and dates from 1953 - 1955. Most of the poems in section 3 had been published in periodicals around 1957. *Howrah Bridge and Other Poems* was organized in similar fashion.

Consequently *In Fires of No Return* provides a quite coherent and full account of the talents of the young Baxter. Three poems in section 2 collected for the first time are particularly interesting: "Seraphion," "Elegy at the Year's End" and "Lament for Barney Flanagan." Never a proponent of art for its own sake (nor, I believe, of the New Critical dogma that art should be considered without reference to its creator), it is nonetheless possible that as late as 1954 Baxter saw art as the supreme human activity, the artist therefore as privileged. From different angles, in each of the three poems mentioned above is a convergence of life and art. "Seraphion," in lines sensuously and wonderfully appropriate, concerns the temptations of the flesh. Seraphion's ultimate temptation takes the form of homosexuality (an underlying concern of Baxter's writing at one time or another). From this same period "Notes Towards an Aesthetic" makes two references to Oscar Wilde, and "Over the Tin Fence" (1955) is "a consideration of the life and work of Oscar Wilde."[11] As this piece shows, Baxter was much interested in the interconnections between artists' lives and their work. Speaking of Wilde and Villon, he makes the important observation that "their work was a creative recognition of precisely those situations which their vices had helped to create."[12] "It may reasonably be said, in objection to any semi-biographical approach to Wilde's art, that his homosexuality is an irrelevant factor; but I disagree.... Wilde's writing, seen as the literary affectation of the lion of a clique, wearies one with interminable egotism; as the expression of the basic social and moral tensions of a man whose experience of the world is irremediably homosexual it assumes an entirely different aspect." (*Numbers*, no. 3, 21 - 22). As Baxter saw it, in Wilde's case the antinomies of life and art were never resolved. Having the misfortune to feel deeply for a person shallower and crueler than himself, Wilde suffered and was immeasurably deepened, with consequences for him as an artist.

Baxter's Seraphion is a different sort. The hermit of Mount Athos, once a "Singer of ballads, thief and actor," isolates himself in a high rock shelter in an attempt to purge himself of sin, praying, "Deliver,/ O Lord, my soul alive!" Once a hedonist, he has now taken to shunning all temporal beauty, having removed also all sexual temptation; but he cannot shake off the memory of Hyakinthos, the "sea boy out of Smyrna," upon whose fleshly charms he dwells, in the deep of night, even though the boy has betrayed him. Splendidly ambiguous and superbly modulated, "Seraphion" tells of the extreme difficulty of purging the flesh. Beneath the efforts at purgation, however, are perhaps Seraphion's unconscious strivings to sustain himself in his own former fullness, to be reborn to it (the boy Hyakinthos is the reborn).

The question is: are not his strivings misdirected? From the unexpurgated *De Profundis*, intrigued by the tension between personal struggle and social pressures, Baxter settles upon

When first I was put into prison some people advised me to try and forget who I was. It was ruinous advice. It is only by realizing what I am that I have found comfort of any kind. Now I am advised by others to try on my release to forget that I have ever been in prison at all. I know that would be equally fatal.... To regret one's own experiences is to arrest one's own development. To deny one's own experiences is to put a lie into the lips of one's own life. It is no less than a denial of the soul. (p. 25)

For Baxter the unique value of *De Profundis* lay precisely in Wilde's recognition as a human being "of a genuine incompatibility between the moral and the aesthetic vision of life," of the split between Orpheus and Prometheus. The notion that Seraphion had completely other concerns may be more apparent than real. At any rate, Baxter felt the same incompatibility in his own experience, but the germ of his ultimate reconciliation of the two is evident in his perception that Wilde grasped "that the moment of aesthetic recognition, in which the artist draws triumphantly upon the undivided powers of flesh and spirit, annulled the moment of repentance" (25).

For much of his subsequent career the split self engaged Baxter's attention as important. In a later *Numbers* he deals with it in a parable of brother princes. One was a paragon: obedient, sharp-witted, intellectually able, endowed with physical prowess, judicious, modest, and serious-minded. His younger brother was an idler in the taverns and red-light districts, and a poet. Dying, the king addresses his elder son: "You will be content in high office and in the possession of a good conscience. He will never be content this side of the grave, for the spirit of turbulence in his heart will reject every custom, law and institution, asking from man and nature an impossible harmony. Yet his songs are the fruit of that harmony, which he knows best by the pain of its absence. He will always jerk against your yoke; and you will always find him hard to bear. But without either of you my kingdom would not be complete...."[13] Never doubting that the artist has some role in the scheme of things, Baxter would in the end find that it could not contain him. Meantime, Robert Chapman made an acute point: "There is a sense in which Mr. Baxter as a romantic wants both the personal enjoyment of chaos and the poetical duty of restoring order."[14]

We come now to Baxter's own equivalent of "The Ballad of Reading Gaol" (Wilde's "one major poem," he says), though Baxter projects the role onto a friend. Wilde's poem he sees as his rejection of his early, Apollonian sense of art, as self-renewing, and his sacrifice of measure and balance to gain "vigour, scope and sincerity." He sees in Wilde's hanged guardsman a projection of himself as "the criminal who through suffering becomes the holy victim, the scapegoat," for the living a Job-like condition (as in Jung's *Answer to Job*). The protagonist in "Lament for Barney Flanagan" lives and suffers, his Dionysian amplitude meriting "the light perpetual":

> Flanagan got up on a Saturday morning,
> Pulled on his pants while the coffee was warming;
> He didn't remember the doctor's warning,
> "Your heart's too big, Mr. Flanagan."

The Door Ajar to Let the Furies Enter

Barney Flanagan, sprung like a frog
From a wet root in an Irish bog —
May his soul escape from the tooth of the dog!
   God have mercy on Flanagan.

Barney Flanagan R.I.P.
Rode to his grave on Hennessey's
Like a bottle-cork boat in the Irish Sea.
   The bell-boy rings for Flanagan.

Barney Flanagan, ripe for a coffin,
Eighteen stone and brandy-rotten,
Patted the housemaid's velvet bottom —
   "Oh, is it you, Mr. Flanagan?"

The sky was bright as a new milk token.
Bill the Bookie and Shellshock Hogan
Waited outside for the pub to open —
   "Good day, Mr. Flanagan."

At noon he was drinking in the lounge bar corner
With a sergeant of police and a racehorse owner
When the Angel of Death looked over his shoulder —
   "Could you spare a moment, Flanagan?"

Oh the deck was cut; the bets were laid;
But the very last card that Barney played
Was the Deadman's Trump, the bullet of Spades —
   "Would you like more air, Mr. Flanagan?"

The priest came running but the priest came late
For Barney was banging at the Pearly Gate.
St. Peter said, "Quiet! You'll have to wait
   For a hundred masses, Flanagan."

The regular boys and the loud accountants
Left their nips and their seven-ounces
As chickens fly when the buzzard pounces —
   "Have you heard about old Flanagan?"

Cold in the parlour Flanagan lay
Like a bride at the end of her marriage day.
The Waterside Workers' band will play
   A brass goodbye to Flanagan.

> While publicans drink their profits still,
> While lawyers flock to be in at the kill,
> While Aussie barmen milk the till
>   We will remember Flanagan.
>
> For Barney had a send-off and no mistake.
> He died like a man for his country's sake;
> And the Governor-General came to his wake.
>   Drink again to Flanagan!
>
> *Despise not, O Lord, the work of Thine own hands*
> *And let light perpetual shine upon him.*

Baxter in this moving and humorous send-off is suggesting that in his own way Flanagan had remained in contact with the "single vision," though almost invariably "Single vision dies" and "Brief is the visiting angel" ("Elegy at the Year's End"; IFN, 39). Another homecoming to the memory of lost Eden and witness of present suffering on the "cross of custom, the marriage bed of knives," "Elegy at the Year's End" points to one contrast:

> Meanwhile on maimed gravestones under the
>   towering fennel
> Moves the bright lizard, sunloved, basking in
>   The moment of animal joy,

lucky possessor of instinctive wisdom, in which (after his own, human fashion) Barney Flanagan had shared.

The final section of *In Fires of No Return* continues the unresolved dialectic, "Sigh to the resurrection thunder." Opening with a prayer "To God the Son" (p. 47), it sustains throughout a note of repentance, a desire to be taught obedience, to wear the figurative sackcloth of "The Clown's Coat," in the belief that "Clown and King, the world's night dumb,/To the same tavern come" (IFN, 50), but the protagonist is caught also in the grip of worldly despair: "There is no end, no end, no end/Of man's grief till the destined night end." Despite continued forays into the small land of "the humpbacked roads and piddling schoolhouse" the convictions deepen that no return to the lost Eden is possible.

The strange figure of Janus, whom the protagonist meets in "Crossing Cook Strait" (IFN, 58 - 59) summarizes for him the "civil calm" which breeds "inward poverty," through the misguided efforts of public men such as "Seddon and Savage, the socialist father",[15] who are crippled versions only of Dionysus, "Amputated in bar rooms, dismembered among wheels." Hence the failure of a society based on "policies made and broken behind locked doors," to which the poets "burning with a wormwood brilliance" are utterly irrelevant, because they do not know the true meaning of love.

For all its brilliant moments, however, the last section of *In Fires of No Return* (the new poems) offers no clear development from earlier work, although a change is astir. Still the engagement with Christianity is not wholly unequivocal; concern for humanity is there, but somehow blurred, and often marginal; also present is continued lament for the lost simplicities of the past. New development is confined largely to the technical level. A new tone is beginning to emerge, which, heard in retrospect, is harsher, stonier, sparser. The rhetorical fullness and richness on display in earlier poems such as "Rocket Show," "The Bay," and even "Elegy at the Year's End" are giving way to a textural spareness evident in the book's title poem, in "Auckland" (that moving tribute to Baxter's troubled friend, the printer R. W. Lowry), and in "At Akitio." Here are the first signs of change which resulted, within a few years, in the gristly directness of *Pig Island Letters*, a directness achieved with no loss of richness. Alongside these signs of what is to come, and making them harder to recognize, are moments of what Weir justly calls baroque rhetoric. The two combined gave some commentators the feeling that Baxter had lost genuine contact with his Muse, but the matter was before too long to become clearer. From this time on, there gradually comes into the foreground Baxter's engagement with "the handsome corpse/That cost so little/To be tidied" (p. 66), his society, which ultimately was to absorb his full attention.

CHAPTER 4

That Wild Interior Island

Men are sleepwalkers by nature. It is part of the result of the Fall of Adam and Eve. We can live for years without knowing we are alive. We can imagine we are secure on a ledge 3 inches wide on the face of a 1,000 ft. precipice. I think a poet is concerned to record, for himself mainly, but also for others, those rare moments when he is alive and awake.

It is the business of a poet, I think, to be destitute as well as honest. He may have money; but he should recognize that it is dirt. He may have prestige, but let him hate it and wear it like an old filthy coat. Then he may be able to stay awake a little better. Love will not harm him, though. It will slice him open like a fish, and hang him up by the heels, and let the sun into his private bag of dreams and idiot ambitions. He will think he is dying when he is just beginning to wake up.[1]

AT "the icy dawn of the sixties," "Baxter seems sadder, more backward looking, more nostalgic" observed Louis Johnson in his 1960 *Poetry Yearbook* editorial. Perhaps because he was being eaten alive by the "boa constrictor" of bureaucracy, Baxter offers in his group of poems in that *Yearbook* a revealing image which occurs several times: "The poet sighing in his cage of mirrors" (in "The Joke"), "The poet in his room of mirrors" ("Song"), "The deepest tunnel leads you down / To a torn and blinded mirror / And the angers of the tomb" ("Sisyphus"). These are images of frustration, and Johnson's comment seems to be very wide of the mark. Two of the poems, certainly, look back to childhood, but this is not their chief point. "The Paper Mask" is intent on the question "how to love?" "An Old Photograph" recalls the Baxter of 1951, and partially with nostalgia, but resolves iteslf in an image which perceives poems as "Imaginings that bait the hook / That drags us up to choke in air." Baxter has arrived at "the middle years" for which are kept the knowledge of man's difficult struggle to find the fragments of his soul and piece them together. Becoming a Catholic convert did not, as he knew it would not, solve that problem but merely brought it more clearly into focus. Belief continues in an original haven to which one may look yearningly, such as is still experienced by the Greenlanders of Thule:

> Thulians prize
> The art of love, and several other things:
>
> A song, a boat, a well-carved walrus tooth.
> Their word for "good" means "one who speaks the truth".
> A race uneducated, raw, uncouth,
> They fish, grow fat, laugh much, and have no kings.
> (Yearbook [1960] 28)

But we who live in "the mountains of transgression," or that afterdinner sleep haunted by uneasy dreams, are in the condition of Sisyphus, on the treadmill, with only occasional brief glimpses of grace.

Evident in Baxter's work of this period is feeling of slow, painful growth, and of enlarging outlook. The blurb of *Howrah Bridge and Other Poems* quotes him: "the first part (of the book) was written some time ago by a man who thought he was a New Zealander; the second part lately, in the past two or three years, by a man who had become, almost unawares, a member of a bigger rougher family. The poems written in India mark this change." We have seen that Baxter organized his first two Oxford books by reprinting poems from already-published books and by adding new work. Distinction between earlier and current work in *Howrah Bridge* is not at first easy to discern, but it is there. Certainly, as Thomas Crawford points out,[2] the supposedly narrower Baxter of the earlier work was very much aware of the "outside" world, of the Greek mythic figures and heroes, the pattern which public events in New Zealand shared with the Western countries, and so on, but the self-professed member of the "bigger family" continued to write of New Zealand sports (boozing, fishing for terakihi, etc.) and of "National Mum and Labour Dad." Yet Baxter is right, there is a significant change, not of content but of attitude.

Evidence of change begins with the "current" poems of *In Fires of No Return*. If one looks for marked change in the Asian poems of

Howrah Bridge, as Mr. Crawford does, one will find little obviously new. At first reading, despite their density of local color, they may seem somewhat disappointing, without new preoccupations or particular insights. Baxter's experiences of gruesome poverty in India led him to condemn social systems based on economic values, but for him this is not especially new, as witness such New Zealand pieces as "A Rope for Harry Fat" (HB, 23). Counterpart and something of a contrast to the Indian poems is his essay "Kilokery and Kalekhan: A study of Indian village life," where he dwells warmly upon the details of simple lives cheerfully accepted, and on the ordered sense of community which contrasts with the dark images of crowded cities cluttered with beings famished or diseased beyond redemption.[3] What is new in the poems is a tone of voice, a sinewy quality which signals the banishment from then on of displays of rhetoric merely for its own sake.

Baxter has been much discussed as a consummate imitator of models (or, as D. C. Walker aptly puts it, "a highly syncretic writer"[4]). More or less beneficent influences in earlier stages had included Auden and MacNeice, Yeats and Hardy. Even a cursory look at the early work shows that Yeats was on the whole a bad influence, Hardy a good one. Weir reminds us of the usually overlooked example of MacNeice whom Baxter himself mentions in his *Recent Poetry* statement. Although for many months he carried around Thomas' *Death and Entrances* and could recite pages of it by rote, he was nonetheless never "taken over" by the Welshman, strong as his effect at one time could be. All the influences mentioned were formative, but a different kind of poet from any of these (and indeed from Baxter himself) now helped him to make a quantum leap in finding his own true voice.

The present writer recalls Baxter's sudden discovery of Durrell, an admiration then difficult to relate to Baxter's "lost garden" romanticism, but one which began in the late 1950s (around the time *The Alexandria Quartet* was published) and continued into the sixties. Writing in 1964, Baxter noted: "Durrell loosens up the chains of association, helping one to avoid heavy aphorisms about Time or God, and keep the eye on the invaluable sensory image."[5] Since Baxter matched a mellifluous and resonant voice with a mental tendency to mellifluence and resonance, this astringency learned from Durrell was a great boon and is a likely source of the change, a shift of consciousness toward a sparser, tauter attitude. The better

That Wild Interior Island

new poems in *Howrah Bridge*, rather than being "a gallimaufry of undigested gobbets" (in Crawford's phrase) manifest the change: ("Hot sun. Lizards frolic / Fly-catching on the black ash / That was green rubbish." Or "Who wakes in moonlight groaning for / The dead to answer. Hears above his head / The cranky shutter clatter loose"). One mark of the new sparer style is the frequent use, from this time on, of the two-line stanza. Apart from the early poems, the Asian poems, and a handful of first-rate ballads (most notably "A Rope for Harry Fat" and "Ballad of Calvary Street") the book's range also encompasses three beautifully realized love poems, "The Apple Tree," "She who is Like the Moon," and "On the Death of Her Body"; in which he both celebrates and mourns the mortal nature of "Your limbs, those passion vines":

> They led me to the mountains beyond pleasure
>
> Where each is not gross body or blank soul
> But a strong harp the wind of genesis
> Makes music in, such resonant music
>
> That I was Adam, loosened by your kiss
> From time's hard bond, and you,
> My love, in the world's first summer stood
>
> Plucking the flowers of the abyss.
>
> (HB, 47)

What Baxter felt imprisoned by was man's schizoid condition in our society, that condition which he felt as "Pig Island" and which later, in the note on *Pig Island Letters*, he does not explain entirely satisfactorily. There he says that the name "Pig Island," vernacularly a reference to the South Island, is employed by him "with a satirical nuance to refer to the whole country" (PIL, vii). Earlier he had made the remark that Denis Glover "knew that life was tough on Pig Island,"[6] and shortly after the publication of *Pig Island Letters* he speaks of "the great white heart of Pig Island, that wild interior island of the mind,"[7] presumably in this instance the precious animistic core of experience, which, for him, had ultimate value. Speaking in Auckland in 1963 he described the primal experience almost in Buddhist terms. Of "the natural paradise," he says it is: "A sense of absolute value in what is happening; a sense of being in relation to other people and to things; a sense of endless possibilities of fruitfulness; and above all, the habit of natural contemplation, of letting the mind rest upon, draw nourishment from, the images of nature perceived as an organic whole — as far as such a condition is possible after the Fall of Man." Baxter has two "starting-points". One is the remembered childhood paradise, the other that "man is a walking grave" (as he puts it in *Pig Island Letters*). In the Auckland talk he had also said, "Every man is a tiger dressed up as a sheep. Man is made for self-knowledge, for spiritual deserts, for wrestling with the problems of the inner life as the tiger is born to eat meat." "Pig Island," then, inward and wild, is itself a schizoid conception. First, it is what the *pakeha* has done to Ao-tea-Roa; second, it is both the "tough" life to which man is condemned and the wrestling ground whereon he must fight for salvation, for the transformation of his mirage-laden desert into the green, well-watered garden.

I Pig Island Letters

One danger in discussing the whole range of a writer's work is that judgment becomes flattened off. First, one *accepts* the subject, one values it (for who would bother to write at length on something for which he had little respect?), then sometimes a sense of commitment may, to one degree or another, mislead. Many good things are available in Baxter's work from the beginning, but it should be emphasized that with *Pig Island Letters* he seems to reach an entirely new level of achievement, especially in the title poem. Old faults, shopworn rhetoric and stock response, still linger, but not importantly. Newly evident is a remarkable conjunction of tautness and freedom.

Dominant is the thirteen-part "Pig Island Letters". It must have occurred to Baxter, since he adopted and developed the form, that the sequence is suited to his particular bent of mind, his tendency to return to, and meditate upon, the same few concerns. Technically influenced both by Lawrence Durrell and Robert Lowell, *Pig Island Letters* is distinctively Baxter's and is, besides, free of the formal stiffness and artificiality of his youthful "Cressida" and the pastiche mauve dolors of *Traveller's Litany*. Most eloquently, it is a weighing and judging born of "experiential knowledge." Intimate in its fundamental strategy, its addressee is Baxter's friend, the novelist Maurice Shadbolt. (They first met in Wellington in the late 1950s, and furthered their friendship in Dunedin, where Baxter succeeded Shadbolt as Burns Fellow.) From this time on, especially, Baxter was to put the verse epistle to good use.

His approach to it gives rise to an initial critical problem. Weir has made the well-founded observation that Baxter is at the center of all his poems (C. K. Stead, too, at one time seemed to feel that a certain subjectivity permeated Baxter's work, in his view undermining it). "He is a man without a mask," Weir says.[8] Although I am inclined to agree with this, I do not believe in the *necessary* separation of "the man who suffers and the mind which creates." Yet I can see the problem. I recall that years ago Smithyman nudged me with the notion that there's no compelling reason why any reader should be interested in one's own little personal life.Obviously I feel somewhat uneasy about it myself, hence my use (overuse, perhaps) of the concept of a "protagonist" in Baxter's poems. Writing more recently than Weir, D. C. Walker has felt free to take the opposite view. He speculates that one possible reason for the affinity between Baxter and Lowell is that they are both Roman Catholic converts, so that each man's work derives power from a framework of spiritual authority. (Owen Leeming, in the same 1971 number of *Landfall*, is of a different opinion and at some pains to show that Baxter's leaning on religious authority undermines his faculty for judging his own work.) Walker goes on to speak of Baxter's "significant" "adoption (or rather, adaptation) of a poetic *persona* in the tradition of Yeats and Lowell: the mask of prophet, martyr, wary survivor in a world of flux and disruption"; he adds a little later, "The title sequence of *Pig Island Letters* was an approach to this method[9]."

Persuasively and attractively argued as it is, how much does Walker's view matter? We are frequently told these days that we all "project" all the time. I believe that. There is often (admittedly, not always) a fine line in distinguishing between a way of seeing oneself and the "adoption. . . of a poetic *persona*." One could belabor the problem at some length, but let us say briefly that Baxter's use of *distance* is not always very sophisticated. In this context he seems, at random, to move into a *persona* and out again. On the whole, I am inclined to agree with Weir. What was it Baxter said in Auckland, "We are all tigers dressed up as sheep"? That will do.

The early sections of "Pig Island Letters" are meditations on the past and (*pace* Smithyman) redolent of autobiographical flashes: of childhood; adolescence in "that bare southern town"; his father's First World War persecution as a conscientious objector;

accompanying Rex Fairburn to the Puhoi pub (shortly before
Fairburn's death in 1957, presumably); Fitz, the barman at the
National Hotel, Wellington (Barney Flanagan), and so on. Later
sections are more purely meditative, preoccupied more theoretically
with middle-age, the implications of the aging process. Even the
early sections are not entirely personal reminiscence. Section 2, for
example, begins with a beautifully turned, melancholic sentence,
"From an old house shaded with macrocarpas/ Rises my malady,"
which most likely refers to the gully farm with its macrocarpa
windbreak — the setting of the early, autobiographical poem "The
Homecoming." The remainder of section 2 is presented as a
generalized picture of a typical Pig Island family, and the warping of
love on Pig Island. Only the last line and a half reverts to the
protagonist, and, in this instance at least, the reference is
unmistakably personal.

In September 1963 Baxter sent Shadbolt a typescript of "The
Landward Farms," an earlier version of section 1 of "Pig Island
Letters." An accompanying letter offered glosses:

> And here is a poem I wrote last night just for you; about Dunedin, saying
> more or less — It's a hell of a place to be in, but perhaps we are most
> ourselves in the jaws of death and hell. And that profoundly negative fury
> symbolised in the coastal weather is for me, I suppose, the dark face of God:
> it can move me when nothing else can. I suppose [. . .] is still down there —
> I hope so, for your sake, for he is a humane bloke, open to everyone's
> feelings — no great virtue in Budapest or Florence, but in Pig Island most
> rare and necessary. The albatross is . . . the sign of guilt . . . and [. . .] is the
> Ancient Mariner par excellence, the banished man, for so he interprets his
> retirement from seminary life to the terrors of several marriages — but the
> albatross is also a genuine Christ-image and the bird that outrides the
> endless storms south of Cape Horn . . . (at) a certain point (a secret point no
> one else can determine) any guilt ceases to be the sign of alienation from
> God and becomes the sign of dereliction, of the state of being-broken, the
> despair that is not despair because God is hidden in it. . . .[10]

He goes on to speak of the "gap" (which he discusses in *The Man on
the Horse*, in "Conversations with an Ancestor") and refers to the
shift in his own consciousness away from too total a dependence on
the aesthetic level of experience:

> Talking of the gap — I think I had to be prepared to tear off the bandages,
> not use the poems as bandages, admit the hollow centre to which writing or
> psycho analysis inevitably leads one. . . . But it is a shift away from the

aesthetic patterning, so dangerous to artists because it leads to idolatry of the work. The blind, the deaf, the dumb, are one's closest companions from then on. . . . The gap is the place where a new self is able to be born. All one can do is to avoid hindering the growth of this strange embryo.

Much of this is touched upon in section 1, where the gap has complex connotations — the unbridgeable distance between oneself and others, the actual world itself, and one's own disconnectedness, and even arrival at the humbling experience of middle-age ("The menopause of the mind. I think of it/ as a little death, practising for the greater"). Crucial is the often-quoted, "Man is a walking grave/ That is where I start from." Of some chronological interest, the month following his letter to Shadbolt Baxter wrote me the letter most of which is used as his statement in *Recent Poetry*, where he says, "There is a spot in the arena to which the fighting bull returns. . . . For me . . . latterly perhaps the hour of death which one looks forward to." This concatenation suggests two things: first, more and more clearly Baxter had begun to center his existence on acceptance of death; second, at around this time he seems to have emerged from a comparatively fallow, or dry, period, to have been blessed with a copious flux of creative energy. "And this," he says, writing in section 1, "the moment of art can never stay"; but the section closes in implying the importance of that moment: "whoever can listen/ Long enough will write again." For him *listening* was an extremely important part of the creative act and of being fully alive.

"Wives in the kitchen seem to smile / As we go into the gap"; from the poem's outset the "kitchen god" (see chapter 7 below) is in attendance. Section 2 invokes that gaunt anima-figure, who reigns supreme in a land where "Love is not valued much." "That brisk gaunt woman in the kitchen" presides over her baffled man, her competent daughter who "Will vote on the side of the bosses," and her moody son, who nurtures a vision of apocalypse but continues his dull daily round in apparent unconcern:

> The man who talks to the masters of Pig Island
> About the love they dread
> Plaits ropes of sand, yet I was born among them
> And will lie some day with their dead.

From "typical" New Zealanders he turns (in section 3) to an apocalyptic vision of Dunedin, opening with a reference to the puritan apologist Richard Baxter (adapted from a quotation sent him by John Weir). His own vision of judgment (at seventeen, at least) was a watery one. The sea was a rich source of allusion for Baxter, benign or terrible. In a later poem, "The Waves" (RW, 84), he remembers that

> The slow language of the waves
> Gave hope of truth to come,
> Wideness, a dark meeting
> With a woman with a body like the moon. . . .

But in the present context it is the surf beyond St. Clair beach which clangs "the dry bell" for the youthful onanist who "made a mother of the keg" and lost his innocence (for once the cliché has a fund of live meaning), "In a room where the wind clattered the blind-cord/ In the bed of a girl with long plaits."

Next is another generalized section (4), contrasting the instinctive, animistic Maori with the camera-toting Kiwi of the present, victim of his own conjured up economy-class Venus, "A skinny wench in jeans with a kea's eye." Section 5 (a weak one) begins as a rather vague recollection of "somebody" long ago who, acting God, destroyed a nest of ants with a burning-glass; and modulates, rather disconnectedly, to: "To learn the tricks of water / From the boathouse keeper's daughter/ Is the task of time" (No solemn explication, but one likes the humorous rhyme!) Sex, politics, and art (sections 6 - 8) are introduced in turn, weighed in the balance against "a belief in bodily truth":

> The hope of the body was coherent love
> As if the water sighing on the shores
> Would penetrate the hardening muscle, loosen
> Whatever had condemned itself in us
>
> (Section 6)

Fairburn in the pub tells them (Baxter and Shadbolt, presumably): "No/ Words make up for what we had in youth"; but there is also what they did not have, and hungered for.

By the end of his life Baxter clearly felt that there was some special grace (I mean the term, if I may, somewhere between its aesthetic and religious connotations, sharing in both, not fully committed to either) — some special grace in failure and destitution. The central section of "Pig Island Letters" (section 7) touches on it:

> This love that heals like a crooked limb
> In each of us, source of our grief,
> Could tell us if we cared to listen, why
> Sons by mayhem, daughters by harlotry
> Pluck down the sky's rage on settled houses.

The seed of true self-knowledge lies in our own self-destructiveness, if only we would "listen." Instead, the creative-destructive waters (in some mystical fashion) carry what we ignore:

> For me it is the weirs that mention
> The love that we destroy
> By long evasion, politics and art,
> And speech that is a kind of contraception. . . .

One risks the phrase "in some mystical fashion," because Baxter is obviously not indulging in mere nature-adulation. As for politics, meditating upon his father's courageous past and what it came to ("And we have seen our strong Antaeus die / In the glass castle of the bureaucracies"), he concludes "unwillingly" that although the impulse to political action may be pure, once followed through it "Becomes the jail it laboured to destroy" (section 8).

In the same society, but at the private level, one is forced to the split between "The poet as family man" and as an incorrigible, scarred "convict self" (section 9), the choice between "death by inches" or by being violently "hung up and flayed." Family man and skull-faced twin, both much in need of friendship, suffer the common fate though still harboring original innocence under the stained layers accumulated on this life's journey; but "no one may enter the tree house/ That hides the bones of a child in the forest of a man" (section 11).

Even the dream of living as "natural man" (section 10) leads only to half-life, for to be human is to be the victim both of vanity and of the "mystery" of living itself. The penultimate section, on "the dark prism" (and prison) of self-love, our inward appetites at war with each other and with us, speaks of the human loves which have "tied us to the wheel," not least perhaps because of the persisting possibility of human hope, of the ideal, of "The face of Beatrice moving in the grove" of that dark wood of selfhood.

Section 13, the conclusion, abandons Beatrice, or rather turns from her, to a broader vision, of Mary. Seeking entrance into Heaven the protagonist pleads with her, and she at first responds: "God's grace has need of man's apology." What has he to say for himself, for he has lost the jewel she gave into his safekeeping? "Only the words: *I thirst*"; and this response gains him admittance, for belief and not virtue is the key (as is shown in the miracles of the Gospels). Yet, is he totally confirmed in that faith? Like the suppliant in Eliot's "Ash Wednesday," who has had his glimpse of paradise in this "place of solitude where three dreams cross," Baxter's protagonist believes in God's grace, pure, mysterious, unexpected:

> Is it like that? At least I know no better;
> After a night of argument
> Mythical, theological, political,
> Somebody has the sense to get a boat
> And row out towards the crayfish rocks
> Where, diving deep, the downward swimmer
> Finds fresh water rising up,
> A mounded water breast, a fountain,
> An invisible tree whose roots cannot be found;
>
> As that wild nymph of water rises
> So does the God in man.

II Other Poems

Much of the feeling of *Pig Island Letters* centers on lack of love, on frustrated lives. A middle-class figure in "A Takapuna Businessman considers his Son's Death in Korea" (p. 32), ponders the pointlessness of his existence, his first wife schizophrenic, their son dead, himself a boozer, and his second wife a nag; "Thoughts of a Remuera Housewife" is another Baxter evocation of Proserpine, this time an unloved tranquillized, middle-aged, middle-class figure harboring illusions about the past. These individual failures, like that of the commercial traveler and putative Samson of "Henley Pub," are regarded as outcomes of the failure of a whole society, which "To a Print of Queen Victoria" (p. 48) suggests is rooted in failure, and which has become "This / dull green land suckled at your / blood's *frigor Anglicanus*, / crowning with a housewife's tally / the void of Empire."

In this terrible society the poet identifies with the "Tomcat," who "cuts across the / zones of the respectable" following his own road, without dignity ("thank god!"), full of sex, and pugnacious rebellion; or (as in "Postman") he is taken by a mood of self-disgust:

> I plod
> up Motueka, Colway,
> Karamu, each cold street a
> dragon, and I stuck inside
> the arse-pipe, a mildewed, slow-
> ly moving turd.
> (PIL, 45)

The sense of inner destitution continues growing. "It isn't simple / To be oneself. The void inside / grows troublesome" (PIL, 21), and being oneself is to "have become a salt-scoured bone / Trembling in the drifted rubble." In "Near Kapiti" the protagonist asks:

> Can
> A temperate love atone
> For what it shuts out? I
> Remember one not boy or man
> Who saw on a wild night, Venus, cut
> by mussels, stagger in
> To share his bed in a fishing hut,
>
> Not minding his stubble, his gruff
> Stammer, or stinking socks,
> For the sake of the destitute love
> Opening what the bible words had shut,
> The flower of sorrow, the flesh's paradox
> (PIL, 23)

Present also, as it is throughout Baxter's later work, (in this case in "East Coast Journey") is an explicit death-wish, whose primary cause is loss of the youthful vivid sense of nature ("Waipatiki Beach"), so that one has arrived at *Nada*, the cold hub, "The absolute unmoving hub," from which the only refuge is in the hollow listening place:

> I did nothing there;
> There was nothing to do but listen to some greater I
> Whose language was silence. Again and again I came
> And was healed of the daftness, the demon in the head
> And the black knot in the thighs, by a silence that
> Accepted all.
> (The Hollow Place, PIL, 31)

The book ends with a sequence on friendship, "Ballad of One Tree Hill," addressed to Bob Lowry, an old friend who had died in a state of personal destitution in 1963 just a few days after Baxter had visited him in Auckland. Baxter felt this death deeply, "Of one who died for lack of love," and one passage of the poem sums up the grim stoic realization of *Pig Island Letters* as a whole:

> The road you trod I tread
> In the footprint of your death,
> Where each may stammer, torn
> By the bull's horn,
> But not blab out the truth,
> That it takes a giant's will
> In the house of the black bull
> To live and breathe at all.
> (PIL, 51)

During the period that Baxter was working on *Pig Island Letters* he translated two poems of Rimbaud: "Seven-Year Old Poet" and "The First Communions." This work, as much as any, serves to show his view of the poet, *poète maudit*. Having discovered himself a poet at seven, he thoroughly shared "the hatred of work behind / The child's bumpy forehead." Rimbaud's attendance upon visions has its parallel in Baxter's listening, but, for the time being at least, Baxter now played a role which he frequently deplored, that of critic. Over the years he had reviewed many books, — in *Landfall, The Listener*, and elsewhere — and often had perceptive things to say about them, usually in a posture of involvement rather than of detachment. His 1954 lectures *The Fire and the Anvil* contained good incidental things, less polished but more penetrating than the earlier *Recent Trends in New Zealand Poetry*. Now, under the impetus of the Burns Fellowship, he put together the autobiographical pieces in *The Man on the Horse*, an indispensible aid in the full reading of much of his poetry. He called this collage of notes "the *corpus* of an unfinished autobiography, which I have no intention whatever of finishing" (MH, 11). Of the five parts, one, "Conversation with an Ancestor," is concerned with "the search for the tree of Jesse, the sense of ancestral continuity, which the modern way of life tends to cut down and destroy" (MH, 10); "The Virgin and the Temptress" examines his poem "Henley Pub," considering the relationship between overtly accepted social conscience, the more deeply rooted natural conscience of the individual, and the community of which he is a member; "Literature and Belief," ponders the relationship between an artist's religious duties and his artistic conscience; the book's title-piece ("The Man on the Horse" is a discussion of "Tam O'Shanter") revels in Baxter's fellow-feeling for Burns' work as an expression of "the struggle of the natural man against that inhuman crystalline vision of the total depravity of the flesh and the rigid holiness of the elect" (MH, 92); "Notes on the Education of a New Zealand Poet," the concluding piece, comprises segments published piecemeal between 1949 and 1964 and deals with the poet's growing up, what he preferred to regard as his "education" rather than the gathering of "qualifications" in institutions of learning.

The Man on the Horse is easy to fault as a single work. Apart from the strong force of its author's personality, it has no unity. Rather is it a source book, full of rich insight and observation, composed typically with a deceptively casual air. Outside his poems, it is our prime firsthand document on "Baxter the poet," its *ad hoc* presentation being characteristic of the man and his sense of the purpose of poetry as expression of "experiential knowledge." Its very occasion, tenure of the Burns Fellowship, afforded him opportunity yet again to warn against "the dangers of compromise between individual thought and the patterns of institutions" (MH, 15). Paradoxically, he maintains, one is both the mainstay of culture and the product of its opposite, "that level of hardship or awareness of moral chaos where the soul is too destitute to be able to lie to itself" (MH, 17), though in distinguishing between bourgeois and bohemian he cautions that "complete adherence to one side or the other is probably fatal for the artist" (MH, 20). Thus, in "Literature and Belief," Catholic institutionalism gives him some qualms when considered in its relation to the artist. Beginning fluently he concludes, in a somewhat rambling address, that *"All art is agnostic. . . . A Catholic artist, like a Catholic scientist, must not go beyond the natural evidence that his life and the world proposes"* (MH, 63), and "Theology interprets what is given; art discovers in each unique event, however imperfectly, the pattern of the hidden One" (MH, 64). Not his final answer for this problem, to be sure, and one that does not bear too close an inspection of its logic. His third address, "The Virgin and the Temptress," will engage us in some detail in chapter 7.

In some respects, "The Man on the Horse," a discussion of Burns' "Tam O'Shanter," is the *exemplum* of what Baxter could achieve in critical analysis, though he does it, not unexpectedly, on his own terms. Of Scottish forebears on both sides and brought up on Burns' poetry, "Tam O'Shanter" is a natural for Baxter, but it also has depth of meaning for him in more immediate personal terms — the struggle of natural man with institutional morality.

"Notes on the Education of a New Zealand Poet" concludes with a poem on Prometheus, seen in what is, for Baxter, a not altogether common perspective as "the Titan Prometheus, principle of the rebellious energy in man that enlarges on order by breaking it and allowing it to re-form in another pattern" (MH, 154).

Aspects of New Zealand Poetry (1967) is the latest and longest statement by Baxter on his country's poetry. Over the years he had become progressively less patient with the "tribal piety" of Curnow, particularly as expressed in the latter's long, urbane, but ultimately wrongheaded introduction to *The Penguin Book of New Zealand Verse*. Still New Zealand's most influential critic, Curnow had played a large part in the "canonization" of R. A. K. Mason. Baxter, with an asperity unusual in him, points out that Mason's verse contains examples of stock response and poor writing for which someone of the later generation, particularly Louis Johnson, would be roundly attacked. Baxter's essay is his chief contribution to the literary war between Allen Curnow and the postwar poets, and may be seen as a not-unfair summing-up, since by 1967 the "war" had largely cooled.

The larger part of *Aspects* lists the characteristics brought to New Zealand poetry by Curnow's generation (usually called "the poets of the thirties") and places them alongside what Baxter believes was added by the postwar generation between about 1949 and 1967. Technically, as he saw it, Curnow's generation provided greater freedom both of verse structure and in the recording of "sensation," and a new, casual adroitness of wit. In substance, that generation accommodated in its work the socialist ethos which evolved from the Labour party's tenure of political power between 1935 and 1949, and also developed "a strong mystique of New Zealand identity" (*Aspects*, 21).

As Baxter sees it, the poets who established themselves during the 1950s effected a "change from a prophetic to a therapeutic view of art"(*Aspects*, 25), a shift from regional to social emphasis, a new use of Maori material, and greater freedom in dealing with erotic themes and experiences. He makes other points, but these are the most important. Many of his contemporaries would have quarreled with the assertion that they see art as therapy, and some, at least, have insisted on describing themselves, at one stage or another, as

That Wild Interior Island

regionalists. *Aspects* remains, however, useful as a corrective to Curnow and a clarification of Baxter's own point of view.

Before publication of the rather odd "selected poems," *The Rock Woman* in 1969, *The Lion Skin*, a group of eleven short poems, was issued by the University of Otago Bibliography Room. Most of the poems deal with the marital relationship, and do so in a discursive way which has the air of self-parody. Once again, as in the cases of *Traveller's Litany* and *The Night Shift*, Baxter had put together as a single work a highly unsatisfactory batch of poems. Looking over the span of his career one discerns an undulating pattern, with periods which suggest a diminished alertness. Perhaps this accounts for the effect of *The Rock Woman*, a disappointing retrospective selection of the work of a quarter of a century.

Less than a quarter of the poems are from Baxter's first three books; nearly half are from *Pig Island Letters*. John Weir suggests that "the most recent poetry included here was probably written in 1965."[11] Baxter has selected some forty-five poems from his earlier work and added eight previously uncollected pieces, and his aim appears to have been to give, predominantly, a sense of social commentary, social criticism, interlarded with religious feeling. Nothing is included from *Beyond the Palisade* and merely a handful of poems from *Blow, Wind of Fruitfulness* and *The Fallen House*, two of the finest single volumes by any New Zealand poet. Baxter introduces the book as "a reasonable sampling of my verse of the past 20 years," but it does not do him justice. One could easily become sidetracked into discussing poems that he "should have" or "might have" included, but perhaps the strong preference for *Pig Island Letters* is a sufficient index of self-judgment *in medias res*. He has apparently eschewed poems of passive repining for the lost garden (though that element of his work is included, in such magnificent pieces as "The Bay" and "Wild Bees") in favor of the more positive stance, his facing "the winter of beginning."

CHAPTER 5

In Quest of the Just City

It is possible without obvious absurdity for our politicians to call our country a Happy Island, in some degree a just one. But poets are different from politicians. . . . I believe that our island is in fact an unjust, unhappy one, where human activity is becoming progressively more meaningless.[1]

FROM very early in his career, Baxter believed that the link between artist and society is close, and necessary. He suggested that "the analogy between the processes of art and the ritual of tribal magic is an exact one. Both enable catharsis by discovering shape in history, thus relieving the isolation of the individual" (*Trends*, 5). He saw the artist as "a cell of good living in a corrupt society" (*Trends*, 18) and could never have agreed with that New Critical shibboleth that an artist's life bears no relevance to the evaluation of his work. Rather, and the final shape of his own life seems to bear it out, he held the Keatsian view that "a man's life of any worth is a continual allegory" and once said of himself, "What happens is either meaningless to me, or else it is mythology" (MH, 122), adding that he mythologized his own life. Throughout his career, and centrally for most of it, he believed that the poet's life and work are inextricably bound together and that poetry, indeed all art, has the function of speaking to man's condition and alleviating that condition.

Much of his work suggests that his human world is experienced as chaos, for which his repeated image is "the lion's den" — thus, in *Pig Island Letters* a poem is "A plank laid over the lion's den." Man's struggle is to reduce chaos to life-giving order, though Baxter does not finally make clear whether, as he sees it, the individual imposes order or simply discovers an order already inherent in nature. Whatever the case, he began by seeing poetry both as the means of individuation and the expression of the journey toward individuation.

A poet of varied moods, modes, and approaches, Baxter by and large is subjective, expressionist; but he is not merely confessional, even though at one stage in his career he admired, and learned from, Robert Lowell. His seminal early reading of Jung confirmed his sense that day-to-day experience has much more than its surface significance, hence his lifelong habit of parable-making and his declaration that consciousness itself can only assimilate "the crises, violations and reconciliations of the spiritual life in mythical form" (MH, 23). Beyond this, he had some sense of himself as part of the flux, process. In *The Fire and the Anvil* he observed that "nearly all poetry is dramatic in character. The catharsis which a reader experiences could not occur if he felt the self that the poem expresses to be entirely actual; rather, the self is a projection of complex associations in the poet's mind, and the poem enables the reader to make the same projection" (p. 48). Given the generally Jungian tendency of his mind, I believe that Baxter here is not adverting to the problem of aesthetic distance but acknowledging his sense of collectivity. He is not "confessional" if only because he sees himself as typical or paradigmatic as well as individual. In some part, too, his mythologizing is exploratory, an attempt to locate and clarify his own archetypes.

Another part is his effort to locate himself in the world. When still very young, he concluded that in searching for the true self, the discovery of a home in nature, identification with a place and a past are vitally necessary. For the *pakeha* New Zealander, peculiar problems arose from the historical fact that *pakeha* society was a transplant from Britain grafted, with incomplete success, onto an already existing native society in the islands of Ao-Tea-Roa. Although the graft was virtually to consume the original plant, the attempt to transport the soil from which it had originally grown was doomed to failure. The artist in such a strangely nurtured "society," which lacked "even the shadow of a folk culture" (*Trends*, 8), was forced into the isolation of unreality.

Still a long way from that all-embracing sensitivity to the Maoris which characterized his last years, Baxter in his midtwenties was already very conscious of the Maori "presence" in New Zealand but saw it only as antithetical to the pioneers' intrusion. The Maoris "had their gods to shield them — we have none" (BP, 7). For the original settlers, "the first forgotten," fate is the "life that knows not life," and "unPolynesian, our deaths are near. / From the hills no dream but death frowns." Yet, curiously, the earliest *pakeha* were to an extent forced to reenact the nomadic stage of establishing a culture, and many artists have attested to the importance in New Zealand consciousness of "the comfortless semi-nomadic existence of the swagger and rabbiter and worker on gold dredges" (*Trends*, 5), not to mention the whaling-men and early missionaries. What intervenes between these early pioneers and present-day New Zealand society is the almost craven emulation of British custom and British education, which continues to exist in "the schizophrenia of the New Zealander who cannot distinguish himself from his grandfather" (*Trends*, 9), and to be part of the consciousness of every New Zealander. Without any show of flag-waving nationalism, Baxter fought this cultural dependence constantly, his method at first being to locate the bad spots in his society and fulminate against them, and later to minister to those who had become victims of the society.

Much of his first book, *Beyond the Palisade*, concerns the natural New Zealand environment, the *pakeha* ancestors failing to make a home there, the land remaining a "cold threshold land" still overshadowed by "the weight of an earlier and prehistoric isolation." Brooding Nature is felt as indifferent or hostile, ground of man's suffering and defeat. This passive, oppressive sense of it continues in *Blow, Wind of Fruitfulness*, but the landscape is more peopled and there are more localized, specifically human experiences. By 1951 Baxter felt clearly that animism is essential to the artist's view of the world, his greatest contribution being the linking of "submerged animism with our immediate affairs." A few years later, in *The Fire and the Anvil*, he declared it the poet's task to lay bare "the animistic pattern which underlies civilized activity" (p. 61).

Animism he took to be characteristic of the child and the primitive, and he believed that poetry's vital force derived from rediscovering and revaluing childhood experience, which was at one with nature in "the paradise of childhood," Eden, the lost garden. In contrast, New Zealand's natural environment was experienced by the *pakeha* intruder as remote, impersonal, indifferent, an obstacle to his material possession of the land. As Charles Brasch once put it, "To New Zealanders, however, nature remains above all the enemy to be subjected by force,"[2] concluding that, "It is less nature than we ourselves, suffering from a form of *hubris* almost world-wide today, who have to be subdued and given a proper sense of our place in the scheme of things." This was Baxter's view also. He, more than any other New Zealand artist, in both his work and his life, labored to achieve that "proper sense."

What brings about the change from the child's animism to adult *hubris* and antinaturism? As Baxter sees it, there are two very different kinds of adult in modern society. These are *natural man* and *bourgeois man*, and each is incomplete. I do not know whether Baxter ever read Hesse, but the distinction he makes is similar to the Steppenwolf/Harry Haller division, although Baxter's "natural man" is a roisterer from the start. Most adults are bourgeois, conscious of a lost freedom, but not nearly conscious enough. Some passages of *The Fire and the Anvil* concern a third category, the intermediate stage between child and man, the adolescent, who "recognizes then for the first and often the last time that he is an individual, a free agent" (p. 52). His "huge discovery" is that freedom is our present condition. Most find the discovery too burdensome and choose instead conformity, but for the few who do not the intermediate stage between child and man becomes a seedtime of creativity. Most turn away from "His flawed mirror," the natural world:

> hiding our souls' dullness
> From that too blinding glass: turn to the gentle
> Dark of our human daydream, child and wife,
> Patience of stone and soil, the lawful city
> Where man may live and no wild trespass
> Of what's eternal shake his grave of time.[3]

Baxter is not totally unsympathetic to this retreat, but it would be a self-betrayal for the artist, or creative man, the one who has embraced his "huge discovery." His role is to provide a health-giving element of rebellion.

Natural man and bourgeois man is each a "half-man," and "the poet as family man" experiences a double portion of Original Sin, for he is conscious of his participation in each half and finds himself involved in a hopeless struggle to integrate the two, though he is instinctively nearer to natural man whom, in the fictitious guise of Timothy Harold Glass, Baxter describes as "the fallen Adam, who remembers, as if in a dream, his first state" (MH, 20).

For the young Baxter a valued experience in this struggle, an embryonic hint of community, is that of friendship, in his own case with Denis Glover, Louis Johnson, Colin McCahon (painter of profound New Zealand "landscapes"), Bob Lowry, the Auckland printer — "Opening his heart like a great door / To poets, lovers, and the houseless poor" — or Fitz, the barman at the National Hotel, Wellington.

Memory of Eden gives the natural man his consciousness of himself as man-beast, and his drive to rebel against the society which otherwise encourages all that is basest in humanity, particularly inertia and indifference. Acedia is the dread affliction to be fought. Baxter states the dichotomy in many poems, such as "At Aramoana":

> I turn also
> to my dream, in nooks below
> the sandhill cone, where Gea
> speaks in parables of rock,
>
> wordless, unconnected with
> the acedia of a tribe
> never *once* happy, never
> at peace. . . .
>   (MH, 24)

Bill Pearson, in a valedictory note just after Baxter's death, recalls a period of friendship in the late 1940s, when the two saw a great deal of each other: "We remembered *Darkness at Noon*, and read Graham Greene, talking in terms no longer in vogue of natural man and original sin and of eros and agape and caritas and the sin of sloth or despair to which he felt especially prone and called by its mediaeval name *accidie*."[4] Since they name the central concerns of his life the terms never became unfashionable for Baxter. In his "Prose Poems" of 1952 we find him petitioning, "Acedia, my mother, when shall I be born? / A thousand times I have lain down in your black swamp, desireless";[5] many years later he will declare, "it is worth remembering that the devil of acedia is the most subtle as well as the most brutal of the masters of Hell" (MH, 15 - 16).

Closely related to "custom," acedia is both cause and symptom of the individual's lack of a tribe. Always deeply conscious of the sufferings of the poor and all kinds of social derelicts, Baxter was yet highly skeptical of socialism and the welfare state as tribal matrices. In answer to the question, "How does this acedia affect the fabric of our society and how does it perpetuate itself?" he would have replied that since New Zealand society (a variation of Western society) is materialistic, secular, and hostile, the individual is without a tribe and consequently lacks life-sustaining *aroha* ("love"), but that the socialist state could not be the ultimate answer. He grew up and came to maturity during a period when the New Zealand Labour party first had clear governmental power (1935 - 1949). To many, that period still seems the finest in New Zealand's brief history. Baxter's father was a socialist sympathizer. Baxter himself, influenced deeply by his father, was yet skeptical of the socialists. They, as much as the National party, in power for most of Baxter's adult life, seemed responsible for the fact that New Zealand society was in his eyes "an unjust, unhappy one where human activity is becoming progressively more meaningless" (*Trends*, 16).

This failure to implement the pioneering dream of establishing a Just City Baxter attributed chiefly to the "spirit of secularism" which he defined in a lecture on "Poetry and Education" as one that

has its own pseudo-sacred canons, derived in the main from the social sciences; which, though deeply hominist, is impatient of individual intuition, fantasy or eccentricity; which adheres vaguely to a notion of inevitable moral progress among mankind; which relies for its evidence on numerical calculations; which regards art as decoration or adornment for the museums and cemeteries of public culture; which regards the State, or agencies of the State, as an ultimate authority superior to tribes, families, religious organizations, or the individual conscience. Belief in it excludes belief in anything beyond it.[6]

Such a matrix led inevitably to sterility and joylessness, and in such circumstances the poet's commitment is to speak out against centralization, depersonalization, and mass conformity. Social criticism began to occupy a central place in Baxter's poetry in the mid-1950s; from that time on he employed the poem as a weapon in dealing with a variety of social problems.

Among his earliest sociocritical poems are those based on the *persona* of Harry Fat, a group in which he makes fine use of his enviable skills as a balladist. One, "A Rope for Harry Fat," is the most effective poem I have seen pleading for the abolition of capital punishment. Another, "The Private Conference of Harry Fat," epitomizes the "virtues" of the secular welfare state — material possessions, anti-intellectualism, hidebound insularity, mindless patriotism, and pseudodemocracy:

> Said Harry Fat, "I've read about
> A doll who liked to sing,
> And when you tapped his wooden head
> His little bell would ring.
> I like the kind of country where
> The little man is king."
>
> "I quite agree," said Holyoake,
> "It is a splendid thing."
>
> Said Harry Fat, "I've heard it said
> The Civil Service needs
> Protection from the Communists
> Who sow rebellious seeds.
> The right man in the right place
> Will pluck them out like weeds."
>
> We must keep watch," said Holyoake,
> "On any man who reads."[7]

Sympathizing as he did with socialist attitudes to welfare economics, Baxter nonetheless felt strongly that state organizations and administration of man's affairs led to dehumanization. Before him he had the example of individual protest by his father and brother, each of whom had been a conscientious objector (one in each of the World Wars). Archibald Baxter, the father, had been physically tortured:

> But he is old now in his apple garden
> And we have seen our strong Antaeus die
> In the glass castle of the bureaucracies
> Robbing our bread of salt. Shall Marx and Christ
> Share beds this side of Jordan? I set now
> Unwillingly these words down:
>
> *Political action in its source is pure,*
> *Human, direct, but in its civil function*
> *Becomes the jail it laboured to destroy.*
>
> (PIL, 10)

Life in the land of "Rev. Fraser" and "Seddon and Savage, the socialist father" is a "civil calm" which "breeds inward poverty/ That chafes for change." The crude impoverished texture of daily existence in the welfare state is wittily, scorchingly captured in "The

Ballad of Calvary Street": "Where two old souls go slowly mad, / National Mum and Labour Dad" (HB, 53), having raised their typical family into the same environment of bored habit and neurotic possibility which has nurtured them.

State secularism had removed even the need for surface religious observance, but it had failed to remove a restrictive puritan outlook which always seemed to him the main enemy of community. In a useful appendix to his Baxter thesis, "Baxter and Puritanism," Weir's starting point is Pearson's classic essay on New Zealand mores, "Fretful Sleepers." Of Puritanism, Pearson says:

> Puritanism runs in a spiral: first its religious context is lost and with it the justification of the restrictions on enjoyment of the senses, it hardens into habit; second, a younger generation rebels and seeks what was forbidden, the thrill of the chase is spiked with a sense of guilt. What they hunt is symbolized in the sex act: but since the pleasure, if isolated, is momentary and the more it's sought the less it can be found, they are tracking down a mirage, and they end in and out of the lupins with this girl and the next one, and have to remind themselves that they did get what they were looking for. When they marry, the men and women of this generation transmit their dissatisfaction to their children, or the children sense it and grow up with a cynical, street-corner dog-like attitude to 'sex': everyone is after it but there's nothing in it. A new austere puritanism grows which is a contempt for love, a sour spirit, a denial of life itself: the puritanism of Graham Greene.[8]

Worry about the effects of this local brand of puritanism is not unique to Baxter among New Zealand writers, and Weir contrasts him with Frank Sargeson: "Baxter would not share Sargeson's conviction that the Just City can be founded solely on humanitarian principles. Accepting the Christian ethic, he must surely resist a meliorist philosophy which does not take account of the Fall. It is from this viewpoint that he described the black frost which follows on 'the falsifying and sterilizing of life by a civilization that tries to pretend there never was a Fall. . . .' "[9] Animadversions against freedom in sex and other areas of experience stem, Baxter felt, not from purity of mind or soul but from what he called (in another letter to Weir, 5 May 1961) "a dreary ethos of fear and prudence." Aspiring writers wishing for social success, he advised, had best ignore "the doctrine of Original Sin, offensive to a society whose wealth and culture is founded on clean refrigeration."[10] In "Elegy at the Year's End" (and many other poems) secular puritanism is perceived as the force behind "what men hold in common, / The cross of custom, the marriage bed of knives":

> Spirit and flesh are sundered
> In the kingdom of no love. Our stunted passions bend
> To serve again familiar social devils.
>
> Brief is the visiting angel. In corridors of hunger
> Our lives entwined suffer the common ill:
> Living and dying, breathing and begetting.
> Meanwhile on maimed gravestones under the towering fennel
> moves the bright lizard, sunloved, basking in
> The moment of animal joy.
>
> (IFN, 39)

Baxter's portrayals of the kingdom of no love, many and penetrating as they are, range from the direct social consciousness of the early "Mill Girl" to such middle pieces as "A Takapuna Businessman Considers his Son's Death in Korea," from the bawdy, cloacal wit of "Ballad of Calvary Street" (where "yin and yang will never meet") to the all-consuming desire for community in late works such as *Jerusalem Daybook*. At eighteen he had experienced the cold hub of nothingness, in a country of emptiness, where (as he put it later)

our pioneer fathers while laying waste the bushland wiped out also the spiritual flora and fauna of Polynesian animism, and replaced it, not, as we might think, with the highest humanist values and the seasonal ritual of the Church, but with Douglas Social Credit and the Women's Christian Temperance Union. In our arts and institutions we have cultivated a narrow ground — political loyalty; business acumen; an admiration (via the Tourist Bureau) of large scenery; the community of the hotel bar and playing field; the Puritan virtues, with their accompanying vices . . . but outside the cultivated area remain unexplored the creative powers of man. (FA, 30 - 31)

Among institutions, the education system was most frequent butt of Baxter's sardonic wit. His work abounds in portraits of frustrated schoolmistresses, mad or malevolent headmasters, and the desolate prisonlike atmosphere of schoolrooms or country schoolhouses. In a late poem, he wrote:

> These poor words are my track to Heaven
> Because they are a gift of sorts
> And may blow in among your thoughts
> Like a fresh wind, where you lie bound
> In that grim dungeon underground,
> The spidery crypt our time has made

> To prove no shovel is a spade, —
> I mean, that graveyard of the nation,
> The oubliette of Education
> Where God's voice calling finds no daughter
> And charity grows thin as water.[11]

Autobiographical passages of *The Man on the Horse* reveal that from the first Baxter resisted formal education, intuitively realizing that it is destructive of individual vital force, and that it interferes with "the discovery of a sacred pattern in natural events" (p. 132) and replaces it with "the lens of abstract thought." This process reaches its culmination in universities with their chimerical exponents of "lean / Philosophies of When and If."

Baxter repeatedly excoriated the education system because it did not answer to the deepest needs of the individual but, on the contrary, tended to denature him. In addition, the system works to perpetuate New Zealand's subservient status, even to the extent of having the children sit in classrooms where "murals represented the English seasons, with lambs and green fields in April" (*Trends*, 6). In this ambience young New Zealanders are indoctrinated in "the Calvinist ethos," taught to subscribe to the work ethic, to distrust sex as evil and all kinds of pleasure as debilitating, and to be career-minded and goal-oriented. A typical parable in "Notes on the Education of a New Zealand Poet" relates an encounter between an Education Department official and an old country Maori. Looking for the right road, coming to a fork, the official asks the old man the right direction.

> "I don't know, boss," said the Maori, "Over the hill somewhere."
> Becoming exasperated, the official says:
> "Look . . . if I don't get to Auckland today I'll miss the beginning of a very important conference. . . . This country needs education, and they need me to make the right plans for it. . . . What's wrong with you, anyway? You're more lost than I am."
> "No, I'm not lost, boss. You see, I'm not going anywhere." (MH, 128 - 29)

Presumably the old Maori's "core of primitive experience" had never been threatened by the education system, a system from which people need to be rescued (Baxter admired A. S. Neill because he felt that Neill's approach was to allow children scope to de-educate, and thus free, themselves). "What kind of education would I have preferred?" he asks. "Perhaps — till ten years old, on a farm in the South Island mountains or the Urewera country, learning to handle a horse or a dog or a gun; then, for a year or two, during puberty, in a Maori *pa*; then perhaps on the coastal boats. . . . But our firms and departments require literate peons for dreary empires of economic liberalism. So we have universal and compulsory education" (MH, 137).

Part of the inward poverty of New Zealand life is an uneasy awareness of "overseas." For perhaps the first hundred years of his country's existence as an independent state, the New Zealander thought of Britain as "Home." Since the generation of the 1930s writers have tried to alter this and have succeeded, but partly at the expense of feeding a neurotic insularity. When Allen Curnow resented and fulminated against "overseas experts" he had in mind Britain and, in particular, the tendency of British visitors to New Zealand to offer lofty advice; but throughout the 1950s and 1960s the fabric of New Zealand's daily life (not exempt from the fate of the rest of the Western world, in spite of its isolation) became progressively more Americanized. In particular, the intervention of the United States in Asian affairs doubly impinged on New Zealand, where the feeling is growing that Asia is not, after all, "the Far East" but is the Near North.

Baxter, who spent a period at school in Britain just before the Second World War and visited India at the end of the 1950s, saw himself positively as a New Zealander, committed fully to life in "Pig Island," but he always refused to be merely nationalistic or to pretend that the fate of New Zealand was somehow different from that of other small, relatively uninfluential Western countries.

The substratum of anti-American feeling which has existed in New Zealand throughout the post-1945 period was given impetus by New Zealand's direct involvement in the Vietnam War. Particularly from early 1965 on, various writers such as Barry Mitcalfe, Hone Tuwhare, and Baxter became immediately and directly involved in antiwar protest at a time when most of the population seemed to be in favor of troops being sent to Vietnam and when street protest was a very uncomfortable business. Baxter issued a number of antiwar ballads, such as "A Bucket of Blood for a Dollar," "a death song for mr mouldybroke," and "The Green Beret." While these poems are not among his best work they were the most effective written contributions to the campaign against New Zealand involvement, and they show Baxter as an active "cell of good living" in the period just before his final total commitment to the ideal of community. At

In Quest of the Just City

the time he said, "The economic liberal Caesar and the communist Caesar, for complex public reasons, are tearing the world apart; in order to die differently, I listen instead to the voice that speaks to me out of the ground. I will never take up arms for any Caesar" (MH, 30). Throughout his career he many times characterized the poet's vocation as listening to the voice of the earth. His voice told him, increasingly, to act.

Baxter's New Zealandness was no simple thing. No isolationist, he rejected the 1930s mystique of Allen Curnow and M. H. Holcroft, who had seen the country as an Island in Time. Baxter was committed to New Zealand first because he happened to be born there and to live there. He felt New Zealand's uniqueness, but he was also aware that it shared most of its social problems with other Western countries. How, we may ask even so, should we interpret Baxter's particular sense of "being a New Zealander" as manifested in his poetry? In one sense this is answered by his work as a whole, in another by his particular conception of "Pig Island" — realm of limited expectations, with its covenant of sheep, farm gear, and sale day drink always within the sound of the vast seas, reminder of human littleness in the scale of nature. "Love is not valued much in Pig Island," but rather its domestic simulacrum — captive demanding wife, husband puzzled as to the origin of his vague frustrations, son and daughter growing in their parents' stunted image; yet for Baxter New Zealand was "the only world I love: / This wilderness." As he saw it, a large part of his vocation was to restore wilderness freedom to the Unjust City of contemporary society.

Throughout the years Baxter's social concern involved many aspects of life in society: drugs, sex, pornography and censorship, the submerged class system, bourgeois conformity. For most of his life there was nothing exceptional in his views on these matters. They were, if one may put it so, conventionally "open" and "liberal," though always with a Christian base. The final years, however, witnessed a notable change, a deepening, which we may sum up with a statement from the concluding essay of his *Six Faces of Love:* "To love means in the long run to die for one's friends. There are no exceptions to that rule."[12] Baxter lived up to this discovery in his work at the Jerusalem Commune which he founded deep in the New Zealand countryside, and in the doss-houses in Auckland and Wellington. The writings of that period are central to our closing chapter.

CHAPTER 6

A Cell of Good Living

There is a spot in the arena to which the fighting bull returns (a different spot for each bull) and from which he comes out more assured and formidable. For me it was once the beaches of the place I grew up in; then the pub; and latterly perhaps the hour of death which one looks forward to. If this spot is correctly located one can generally go on writing.[1]

IN a well-known early poem Baxter said of his father, "behind slow speech and quiet eye / The rock of passionate integrity. / / You were a poet whom the time betrayed / To action" (FH, 14). If Baxter has a vision of the good man, the hero, perhaps "passionate integrity" is that figure's chief virtue? Early in *Love and Will* Rollo May writes of the individual's need to accept a "schizoid" condition in order to survive in modern Western society. What May was pointing to, of course, is the deep split between professed Western ideals and the conduct of individuals in our society. Baxter may well have thought that survival on such conditions, consciously accepted, was worthless; but believing as he did that man was born in some sense schizoid — the creature with his feet in the mire and his head among the stars — he had to face the question of how such a one could be "a cell of good living"?

Some of the young Baxter's poems evoke the particular characteristics of New Zealand: mobs of sheep, beer-drinking, "the earth-wave breaking / to the plough," and the life-rhythm of the slow-thinking, sandy-haired farmhand with his sun-scorched face:

> But ah in harvest watch him
> Forking stooks, effortless and strong —
> Or listening like a lover to the song
> Clear, without fault, of a new tractor-engine
> (BWF, 51)

A Cell of Good Living

Similarly evoked are the social pieties implied by "Elegy for an Unknown Soldier":

> So when the War came he was glad and sorry,
> But soon enlisted. Then his mother cried
> A little, and his father boasted how
> He'd let him go, though needed for the farm.
>
> Likely in Egypt he would find out something
> About himself, if flies and drunkenness
> And deadly heat could tell him much — until
> In his first battle a shell splinter caught him.
>
> So crown him with memorial bronze among
> The older dead, child of a mountainous island.
> Wings of a tarnished victory shadow him
> Who born of silence has burned back to silence.
> (FH, 12 - 13)

Such poems capture neatly enough the innocence of a young man who does not know himself, scion of a land spiritually and historically impoverished and yet obscurely felt to be his, and behind this the double inarticulateness, of the man and of the land itself. Baxter never ceased, in some measure and in some part of himself, to share these pieties; but it was not his, nor his hero's, fate to remain "effortless and strong." Nor did he need go to Egypt to "find out something / About himself." What he discovered he began to discover early and it haunted him. At first intermittent, these were early glimpses of the desperate absence of, and desperate need for, *agape* — a lack which he felt was importantly at the center of his own experience and that of his society.

I *Odysseus*

All walking, or wandering, is from mother, to mother, in mother; it gets us nowhere.
Norman O. Brown, *Love's Body*

"Farmhand" and "Elegy for an Unknown Soldier" are not typical of Baxter's early work, or of his work as a whole. Much more so is "The Homecoming" (PU, 21), with its Odysseus "come home to the gully farm" in which the mother-figure is both psychologically and emblematically real. Baxter's protagonist is on a journey, but on this journey the *return* seems as important as the outward movement: "Ithaca is your remorse, / The home each sailor loves and runs away from" (*Yearbook* [1953], 61 - 65, "The Sirens"). In a slightly later piece, "Odysseus," the poet again seems to perceive journey and return as emblematic of the necessary compromise resulting from man's schizoid condition. Youth's fire seems to produce "War, love: habits you invented / And left like blackened oven stones," but "the second life" denies original force, for

> Burying your salt sperm
> In the cupboards of a grum wife.
>
> Only the eye remains
> Under a hairy porch:
> "I *was* Odysseus."
> Eyes of a gull follow a gull
> From a terrace by the sea,
> Considering the true bride, Freedom,
> Oar-holes worn large, a voyage to no harbour,
>
> Youth abandoned for a labouring star.
> (*Yearbook* [1957 - 58], 17)

This Odysseus is the self-making or self-sustaining ego which, periodically at least, is forced to encounter the world other than itself. Clinging to him is the desire to remain (in Norman O. Brown's term) in "the cave of separateness," withdrawn into selfhood; but implicit in the very choice of Odysseus as protagonist is acceptance of the encounter. Terrifying it may be, necessitating repeated withdrawals, but the drive to venture from the cave of being is stronger than the desire to remain dormant (though at the other end of Baxter's life there are repeated signs of the reversal of this condition).

Yet another Odysseus poem, "The Journey," takes the situation at the end of book 10 of the *Odyssey:*

> Homeward you think we must be sailing
> to our own land; no, elsewhere is the voyage
> Kirke has laid upon me. We must go
> to the cold homes of Death and pale Persephone
> to hear Teiresias tell of time to come.[2]

A Cell of Good Living

A fine example of what Smithyman calls Baxter's "high ritual speech," "The Journey" is surprisingly not one of his better-known poems:

> Then, coming to the long ship, they stowed
> Wineskins aboard, water from the sedgy creek,
> With red apples, honey from the wild bees' hoard
> By shepherds ransacked from a raven's cleft
> Where ivies tomb the twilight and the spider keeps
> Vigil yearlong. All these, gifts of the goddess, were lashed
> Under the rowers' benches — the bellowing ram also
> And black ewe, on whose fleece the flung saltflake dies.
>
> With handclasp, singing, and shed tears they take
> Leave of Aeaea, the green isle summer-browed,
> Isle of their drowsy feasting. With the sound of *never*,
> The keel rasped on sand, rode, rocked on the greymaned wave.
> Moaning and manybreasted, the whale's path lay
> Westward, perilous, to Cimmeria the sunless
> And Hades' silence. All eyes looked back.
> Only Odysseus, in the ship's prow standing, did not turn or speak.
>
> And like a stormbird through daylight and darkness
> She fled, a serpent wake behind her coiling,
> The sun a broken shield, or clammy nightfogs drifting,
> Till at the frontiers of the murmuring Dead
> They beached, where poplar and lamenting willow
> Let fall their vacant seed. There made
> Sacrifice to Persephone, sprinkled the white barley.
> The Dead gathered, like moths, with wrath and ululation.
>
> (HB, 17)

Evoked here is the descent into underworld darkness which precedes second birth or full birth. Another poem from the same period opens:

> Dark the cave. Broken the rock hymen.
>   Night of the world at my door,
> Uncover, uncover the grey locks of the gorgon
>   But let love endure.
>   (*Yearbook* [1957 - 58], 16)

His Odyssean protagonist in such poems appears to be beginning a stage in his spiritual journey. As Joseph Campbell says in *The Hero*

With a Thousand Faces: "if anyone — in whatever society — undertakes for himself the perilous journey into the darkness by descending, either intentionally or unintentionally, into the crooked lanes of his own spiritual labyrinth, he soon finds himself in a landscape of symbolical figures (any one of which may swallow him).... this is the second stage of the Way, that of 'the purification of the self....' "[3] "The Tempter," also in *Howrah Bridge* and seemingly a counterpart to "Odysseus," concludes with instructions for such purification: "A pedlar's maxim: *Thirst, obey, endure*" (p. 41).

But the further eventuality is the return, integral to the Odyssean version of the journey, the return home. In much of Baxter this centers on the complexities of seeing again or remembering the home farm, the stab of recollection at encountering scenes of childhood's lost Eden, the resulting intimations of mortality and duty:

> Came to the rock, asking forgiveness,
> To humpbacked roads and the piddling schoolhouse....
>
> Many miles from here my youth died
> In northern warrens, stifled by invisible
> Cloths of delirium and habitual greed
> (IFN, 61, "The Return")

A more harrowing treatment of the same theme is "The Rocks," apparently from the 1950s but recently published in *The Labyrinth*, which echoes Eliot's work of the early 1920s and deftly reverses the story of the forbidden fruit:

> If I were to pluck and bite
> One hard berry the taste might bring me
>
> Out of the flame in which I burn,
> And the touch of it on the tongue might bring back
> The power of human speech. If the master of the flame
> Would let me, I would gather from the tree at the gate
> Where few go out, a leaf to cool my head,
> And come back darkly at nightfall.
> (p. 54)

In *The Man on the Horse* we may find the counter to this quest-figure in another of Baxter's destitutes, Pete the drunken sailor, and black sheep, who declares "I'm married to the sea," and who finds the rhythm of his life in the voyage itself, like the old Maori who had

A Cell of Good Living

no destination. Pete contrasts also with the witch-ridden commercial traveler of "Henley Pub," for he is able to maintain a proper distance from his women.

Baxter was eventually to deal with Odysseus at some length in his play *The Sore-Footed Man* (1967), which is considered in some detail in chapter 8. Concerned with interaction between Odysseus and Philoctetes the play shows that, later in his career, Baxter's sense of the Odysseus figure had changed somewhat. What concerns us directly here, however, are some introductory remarks:

> Odysseus became in a sense the main character in my own play, since he alone has the power to liberate Philoctetes from his intellectual roundabout. He does, inevitably by stratagem. I trust I have not made him a neo-Fascist. The character of Odysseus had in fact haunted me for many years, from the time I began to realise that neither conventional ethics nor the theology of Aquinas were much use in determining what choices a man should make who wishes to win a war, or court a woman, or even free himself from the chains of family conditioning. I suspect that THE SORE-FOOTED MAN is mainly written around the enigma of human freedom. . . . Odysseus derives his sanction from the unknown fertilising power of action itself. (p. viii)

II *Prometheus*

"Prometheus bleeding on the cross of time" is (in a sense) a more conventional though equally ambiguous version of the Baxter hero. Choosing to conclude *The Man on the Horse* with a Prometheus poem, he sees in the Titan the "principle of the rebellious energy in man that enlarges our order by breaking it and allowing it to reform in another pattern" (MH, 154), beginning so by lightening our chaos through fire but otherwise being, like that "mechanic of an old fraternity" Sisyphus, committed to the human treadmill, grimly existential. Described in "Notes Towards an Aesthetic" as "father of all technicians," Prometheus is antithetical to the singer, Orpheus — they are the two halves of the split man. When Eurydice is left in Hades, Orpheus *feels* for their common wife, while Prometheus attempts to fashion a replacement. Orpheus sings of freedom; Prometheus stresses morality. Orpheus charms the Furies; Prometheus installs them in state-established brothels. Orpheus knows "the pain of separation from the inward bride," whereas Prometheus is deluded in thinking his technical gifts are substitutes for such pain. Orpheus relies on Prometheus for subsistence, Prometheus on Orpheus for "culture." "Each man is both Orpheus and Prometheus. No man has ever yet successfully played one role without botching the other." Given such a division, Baxter's natural sympathies would be with Orpheus. His poem on Hart Crane shows him aware that the poet's Orphic celebrations of Promethean feats are his own doom song:

> This poet, fallen in love with a steel robot,
> Drinking bad whisky in New York for years,
> Wrung out catharsis in a urinal
> And public poetry from private fears.
>
> So pity him, that mining the black gold
> Of prophecy, he dug his own grave.
> Marshfire by night and at full noon the cold
> Vertiginous terror of the buried alive.
>
> And praise him who for the new Birdman built
> That rainbow bridge which only gods can walk
> (Forgetting the dark river underneath. . . .
> (FH, 17)

Odysseus' questing spirit is combined with the efficiency of Prometheus in "Perseus," a not highly successful recounting of Perseus' encounter with Medusa and, under the protection of Athene, his defeat and killing of the gorgon. Athene (Minerva, the virgin goddess) is goddess both of thunderclouds and of wisdom. Part of the poem's thrust concerns the defeat of the witch-figure by the virgin-figure, but the ultimate point is that the encounter with the gorgon results in a somewhat flat return to daily life's "responsibility":

> To earth, Andromeda, the palace garden
> His parents bickered in, plainsong of harvest —
> To the lawgiver's boredom, rendering
> (The task accomplished) back to benignant Hermes
> And holy Athene goods not his own, the borrowed
> Sandals of courage and the shield of art.
> (HB, 19)

III *Samson*

From start to finish Baxter's work is permeated with biblical allusion. Many of the references to Adam tend to portray him as the type-figure of unfallen man, content yet in Eden, to whose company one prays to return and in "Leisure to stroll and see Him un-

A Cell of Good Living

afraid/Who walked with Adam once in the green shade." More like Prometheus, and a more active figure in Baxter's world, is Samson, kin not to Prometheus the fixer but to the blinded Titan, steeped in what Yeats called "the fury and the mire of human veins" yet ultimately more than human. In *The Fire and the Anvil*, Baxter speaks of the special significance of "the exultation of Samson, who involves in his own death the civilization which has blinded him. . . . such exultation is anathema to the social conscience . . ." (FA, 21). But what struck him most deeply was "that tale of Samson's youth / When the dead lion's bones brought honey forth" (FH, 39). He returned to it many times. For example, in "Henley Pub":

> In Father Hogan's box
> I gripped the lion by the jowls,
> Splitting her sin from mine to feed the fowls
> Of judgment. Then wild bees among the rocks
> Loaded miraculous honey in the white
> Carcass.
>
> (MH, 69)

Some critics have found Baxter's own discussion of this poem in *The Man on the Horse* not wholly satisfactory, but in terms of his repeated use of the Samson material it is most illuminating.

He explains that, in the context, Delilah is both witch and darkness. She is also sin or Satan: "The lion is a familiar Christian symbol for Satan; in the poem it signifies rather sin itself" (MH, 79 - 80). The poem begins by evoking the protagonist's general state of burning, with liquor and sexual desire and the knowledge of his own mortality, which even the Mother cannot mitigate. Addressing Delilah he declares, "Your body is my Hell," though Baxter's commentary suggests that he had in mind St. Augustine's words *Etiam peccata serviunt* ("Our faults also are of use"). A central Baxter attitude, this is not clearly brought into the texture of the poem (which may be said to fail on that account) and seems to be contradicted by the closing: "What is a man, this glittering dung-fed fly / Who burrows in foul earth?" Yet the image of the lion skin almost suffices for his intention of suggesting sin as the source of sweetness and goodness, and it can be made to do so through links with his other work. For example, in the first "Letter to Noel Ginn" (BP, 37), "the empty lion-skin" implies meaningless existence, one human choice being seen as persistence without significance. The other (the one touched upon in "Henley Pub" presumably) is invoked in "For Kevin Ireland," which heads section 2 of *Howrah Bridge:*

> Friend, if you have strength to praise
> The lion-headed incubus
> That grips your life and mine within
> Its strict Egyptian maze,
> Expect no lessening of pain. . . .
> (p. 27)

The ancient Egyptians had many lion-headed gods and goddesses, some personifying the destructive power. In the underworld lion-headed deities guarded some of the halls and pylons, and the lion's connection with the dead is obvious in that the head of the bier was always made in the form of a lion's head, the foot of it sometimes decorated with a lion's tail. What is implied in this poem is acceptance of the element of death-in-life, or the paradox that death and life contain each other.

That curious small collection *The Lion Skin* takes the lion's death as its governing metaphor, with the protagonist as Samson. Although most of the poems here concern marriage, the group opens and closes on the theme of drunkenness, and the lion skin may be seen as the whole urban way of life. His Muse has deserted the protagonist because of his civility, his lack of Dionysian fire, and "the city has spread her nets," though he has escaped them. He witnesses an encounter between "a drunk with unlaced shoe" and a nagging woman (the Muse "unhinged by our civility"?). In the succession of poems he celebrates freedom from his wife, to be "Marvellously doing nothing," escape from temptation by her sex, and welcomes "Baron Saturday" ("Having need of his strength, the skin of a dead lion"), his dark side, to escape the deadening effects of "the town whose ladders are made of coffin wood." A strain of so-called "male chauvinism" characterizes the poems; in "Divorcee," for example, where the subject feels, "Better any man / Than the red hot pike of solitude / Thrusting and twisting," and in "The Inflammable Woman" and "A Question of Rape." In contrast, "The Perfect Wife" is another celebration of a man's escape from the female paragon, to emerge "Drunk, dirty, celibate, having seen the light." Town and woman (temple and Delilah) are throughout aligned with death, so that the antisocial states of drunkenness and dirtiness are

A Cell of Good Living

seen along with celibacy as complementary virtues in the context of a life it is "best of all to lose."

IV Barney Flanagan

The three poems which close *The Lion Skin* all concern the "problem" of drunkenness, a means of vulnerability. In one the nurse taking a bloodtest with a syringe becomes a vampire:

> And asks me, "Do you have palpitations?
> Have you put on weight ?" — then pours the blood
> Into two containers, labels it,
> And sends me on my way an inch shorter.

Another, "Fitz Drives Home the Spigot," focuses on a Baxter hero-figure comparable with Odysseus or Samson but more obviously peccable than either. "Fitz," the barman, serves to link the idea of drunkenness with our sexually puritanical society's constant fear of the assault upon female virtue (one of the symptoms of our paranoia) and on its own "Monotonous man-killing identity," its fright

> That the black bones of Dionysus
> Buried under the Fire Assurance Building
> Had sprouted a million wild green vines
> Cracking the pavements and gravestones —

Ranging from the figure of Tantalus ("a moral bankrupt. Knowing better, he must mourn / At his own funeral, pissing against the headstone")[4] to his long anatomizing of the subject in *The Flowering Cross*,[5] the alcoholic figure ("an alcoholic, grave-robbing friend of mine") was his primary version of the victim or destitute hero. Such a one is Mr. Gallonguts:

> "Quite early in the morning
> I have a little snort,
> At midday for my stomach's sake
> A brandy laced with port.
>
> "By gyroscopic action
> At midnight I grog on,
> Though the host eyes the clock and sighs
> And all the guests have gone.

> "I've solved the Sphinx's problem
> Of fate against freewill.
> My thirst is metaphysical
> And craves a heavenly still."
>
> God grant that Mr. Gallonguts
> May suck an angel's nipple
> For he lies long in Avondale*
> And water is his tipple.
>
> (HB, 40)

Another, more significant frequenter of Baxter's world — one who became central in his play *The Band Rotunda* — is "Concrete Grady, an elderly mythical alcoholic of the Catholic persuasion, who often fits the keystone to the arch of a poem for me, (and who) left these few lines with me. . . ."

> The Trinity inside my head
> Is blacked out when they pull the switch.
> I met Bill Diamond in the yard
> And asked him for a match.
> There's fire in Heaven. Through the bars
> I see burnt patches in the wheatfield of the stars. 6

In both cases, and they are typical, the private vision has been reduced or scorched out because of social imperatives. Such a character Baxter sees as being Jonah-like, in the whale's belly, or like Noah, attempting to pack all the animals aboard the ark without sinking it. Alcoholism he recognized as an affliction, but appears to regard it as parallel to, or even an enlargement of, the affliction of being alive and being human, as though it were the human lot to fumble "like ferrets in a sack."

V Man Alone

Examining the various facets of the Baxter "hero" is, in a sense, a way of approaching his themes and a way of recognizing that man is at the center of every one of them. As we have seen, he was conscious of the "traditional" New Zealand figure of "man alone" which he discusses at some length in *The Fire and the Anvil*. Typically he sees the figure as hobo or social outcast, who is sensitive to the need for

---

*Avondale is a New Zealand mental hospital.

"single vision," unifying love, and who is driven by that sensitivity, his isolation forced upon him by his inability to respond to pressure to conform socially. "Man alone" is the artist *sans* artistic capacities, and the artist, because he has made the same discoveries about the crudity of social stereotypes, will sympathize with the "man alone." More common to Baxter's poems of the forties and fifties than afterward, the figure may be found in "Prospector," "The Doll," and "The Hermit," all in *The Fallen House*. In a later, somewhat scatological broadsheet, "The Old Earth Closet" (subtitled "a tribute to regional poetry"), he sums up:

> Across the hills of manuka
> I watched the cows come home
> And as they wandered up the track
> It turned my heart to stone
> That I was a New Zealander
> And therefore Man Alone.

Available evidence cannot make it conclusive either way, but a sly or ambivalent note in this piece suggests that Baxter saw the danger of accepting a type-figure too easily, even though his own sense of the human situation shared in it.

Usually Baxter's hero, "my collaborator, my schizophrenic twin," was no solitary drinker, but rather, like his fictional hero Timothy Harold Glass, or "Horse," "is frequently being ridden by everybody he knows" (MH, 17). Glass is "natural man," who may have picked up his nickname from Jung who, in *Modern Man in Search of a Soul*, cites that animal as figure of the instinctive and antirational. Seen as a half-man (so Baxter professes, although one does not entirely believe him in this instance), Horse is carrier of those "sexual, aggressive and anarchistic motives which enter uneasily the drawing-room of verse" bringing "agonies, desires and dilemmas which the housewifely mind has cast out on the rubbish-heap" (FA, 23). Chameleon-like Horse may be compared with the "gigantic One-eyed coal-black demoniacal" subject of "Tomcat," who, "cuts across the/zones of the respectable/through fences, walls, following/other routes, his own" (PIL, 42). Both imply the social context and, in a sense, revel in it.

VI The Destitute

Perhaps the real heroes, the real center, of Baxter's work are the destitute. He has told us that what he most valued about Denis

Glover was a sense of the older poet's destitution, and we shall see how in the Jerusalem period destitution comes to be, for Baxter, the very essence of the human. His sense of his own destitution came to him early, remained, and grew. "I am generally much more at home in the desert . . . . Destitution can become one's ordinary state," he once said, and image and attitude are found together quite early, as in the pastiche of "Canticle of the Desert" (*Yearbook*, 1955):

> Delusion, mirage of the thirsty
> who strain green sedges from the fingered sand!
> Return, if there can be return,
> is to a waste orchard
> clay sods and ragged thistle
> from the mossed apple bough one purgatorial song.
> Fellow-demoniac
> I will be plain with you.
> These bandages can heal no wound.
>
> (p. 22)

Contemporary society, he felt, is joined by the mere illusion of togetherness, but the necessary condition for struggle toward truth is solitude without separation. In a parable in *Review'67* he tells of a boy who grew up in a house which had an inner room entered by no one (or, at least, no one who would admit to entering it). As the boy discovered, this room contained the shaft of a deep well. He learned much from meditating upon it. Later, marrying, he built his own house and found a similar spot in it. Ultimate cause and significance of destitution, this spot is the black hole, the final tunnel, of mortality.[7]

One such destitute is the Maori Te Whiu in "A Rope for Harry Fat" (HB, 23), a young man hanged for committing a panic killing after a petty theft resulting from poverty, and therefore in Baxter's eyes a victim of society's illusions and consequent cruelty. Another is Seamas, in *The Man on the Horse*, a drunken outcast who slept where he could, "suffering from most of the troubles which a man can stumble into — girlfriend trouble, trouble with the drink, trouble with the police, landlady trouble, trouble with money, and a touch of mental disorder to crown it all" (MH, 45). From just such a destitute Baxter by his own account learned a crucial lesson, for Seamas "had no religious troubles whatsoever" and "wore his Faith like a well-fitting overcoat." By social standards he lacked virtue, but he had belief, which is much more important. An early poem, "Lazarus" (FH, 32), makes the ultimate link between total destitution and faith, faith in a "love, more to be feared than wrath." Much later, in "Poem Against Comfort," it is stated thus:

> We have to strip
> To the bone and beyond before the gate can open
> And our silence be united both to what we leave
> And to the dark centre of the sun.[8]

Early and late Baxter had discovered there is an essential comradeship available among the unfortunate:

In Mother Crawford's boarding house the company is grand,
There's bludgers, thieves and con men who will take you by the hand,
A bloody sight more human than the company outside,
And very very seldom are you taken for a ride.[9]

As "Mother Crawford's boarding house" is actually Mount Crawford jail in Wellington, the lines are a fair illustration of the danger of Baxter's falling into a sentimental attitude toward crime and offenses against social and moral taboo. Not unnaturally, he does not altogether avoid it; but he was to discover again, in the late stages of his spiritual journey, this fellowship of the down-and-out. Yet the possibilities in such a bond did not deceive him. In "To a Travelling Friend" (RW, 30), he asks and answers the pertinent question:

> Where do the rough boys end? In furnished rooms
> Many drink hemlock. Some, some
> Lie like straws in ice, lulled
> By the spider-headed queen.

VII Poet as Hero

The "sore thumb of the tribe", Baxter called him, or more graphically, "a donkey who is able from time to time to excrete gold" (MH, 13), an ability which makes him "a cell of good living in a corrupt society." A tribesman cut off from his tribe by a peculiar and special gap, he is the *revealer* of what lies under the surface, or one who discovers in his cage of mirrors facets of the unexpected and lays bare human depths for all to see.

His type of the poet-hero is Burns, a poet his father read aloud to him and whose work the young Baxter learned by heart before he was six years old. For him Burns was a superbly energetic fighter against Calvinist puritanism, the denatured vestiges of which lay at the withered root of the New Zealand social experiment. Burns, for Baxter, was the poet as natural man, or, rather, in whose consciousness natural man fought hard to hold off the strait-jacket of respectable burgherdom. Not conformity to social mores, not being a "concerned citizen" offering his contribution to maintenance of the status quo, but recognizing the true nature of his own selfhood and the selfhoods of others — this is what Baxter meant by "a cell of good living," and this spirit governs the whole presentation of "The Man On the Horse," his fine exegesis of "Tam O'Shanter" and apologia for the life and work of Burns.

Nevertheless he came to feel that poets must "learn to live like other men," bridging the gap, waiting for the "moment of art" which "can never stay" (or which, in Robert Frost's phrase, is at best "a momentary stay against confusion") and is, in any case, less than the given:

> For me it is the weirs that mention
> The love that we destroy
> By long evasion, politics and art,
> And speech that is a kind of contraception.
> (PIL, 9)

Yet it is the poet who survives a sense of his own crippled and crippling humanity, carrying "the seed of fire," whose vocation it is to set a bound to chaos:

> Look at the simple caption of success,
> The poet as family man,
> Head between thumbs at mass, nailing a trolley,
> Letting the tomcat in:
> Then turn the hourglass over, find the other
> Convict self, incorrigible, scarred
> With what the bottle and the sex games taught,
> The black triangle, the whips of sin.
> The first gets all his meat from the skull-faced twin,
> Sharpening a dagger out of a spoon,
> Struggling to speak through the gaps of a poem:
> When both can make a third my work is done.
> (PIL, 11)

VIII *Tribal Man*

References throughout his work to friends — to Bob Lowry "Opening his heart like a great door," to "How much we needed friends / Like Fitz the barman at the National," to Colin McCahon, Louis Johnson, Maurice Shadbolt, and others (including friends in spiritual life such as Colin Durning and Eugene O'Sullivan) — show how great a value Baxter placed on friendship. Eventually this was to grow for him into the central heroic quality *aroha* — the power of love, the capacity to forget self and put all the force of one's being into a concern for "Thou."

Recent years have witnessed a revival, in works such as Gary Snyder's *Earth House Hold*, and especially since a famous "gathering of the tribes" in California in the early 1960s, of the felt need for tribal man and the desire to reestablish a tribal base in our society. Such a desire was central to Baxter throughout his life, as is evident from "The First Forgotten," for example, in *Beyond the Palisade*, or in his statements in *Recent Trends*. In the late work, from *Pig Island Letters* onward, it becomes the dominating consideration. The tribe is what is lost; the artist "a tribesman left over from the dissolution of the tribes" (MH, 12). Carried forward into the era of social man, and into the conduct of his own life, this will to restore the tribe stems directly from the Edenic vision. In childhood, the Eden-time, Baxter used to imagine "a secret tribe of friends and lovers." Later his hero, though veering toward the savage self-indulgence catered by "Baron Saturday," will be haunted by the loss of *aroha*, and when he girds himself up his whole soul will be devoted to the search for it.

A sense of loss, as Weir valuably demonstrates, is at the core of Baxter, and, in consequence, his hero is a seeker, be it for "The wild lost city of a mother's love," "the bay that never was," or the wholeness all too briefly glimpsed in childhood. From this lost "single vision" the human being is apparently condemned to traverse the "black swamp" of adolescence, to survive the death of "the first Adam" in himself, and to mourn for his "lost estate." Somewhere within himself the hero carries a vision of fullness and this vision is an element in his very destitution: "We give love, and the way the world is jointed causes us to work not good thus, but ill,"[10] for ours is "the fallen heart that does not cease to fall." Perhaps the strongest features of Baxter's work are portrayals of Fallen Man, possessor of a vision which seemingly can never be attained, whose "doomed flesh answers an undying summer," whose "civil calm breeds inward poverty," who is "The Not-Yet-Made." Children "lost in their tribal games" are the nearest human answer to the vision of what is lost:

> In packed ground the missionary fathers
> Drowned at river crossings, rest in one bed,
> While a boy cuts from flax a spirit boat
> Perfect, lightly as a bird's wing
> Riding the void of waters
> Untaught, a full hour floating.
>
> (IFN, 64)

Whereas in his early work Baxter lamented man's loss of the capacity to float untutored on the waters of Chaos, later an acceptance of that loss and a search for comradeship in loss clearly became his protagonist's goals. Beyond that, in the late work, is the acceptance of, indeed the looking for, death. In Freudian terms the early longing for lost childhood and the late willingness for death derive ultimately from the same source — the tendency of all living things to return to an inorganic state. From *Pig Island Letters* onward Baxter seems to hold that, in his journey, the individual must learn to accept the reality of his own personal death.

Because he was so profoundly religious a person there is a presence in much of Baxter's writing of the Christian godhead, but he does not especially make Christ a hero-figure in his work. Had he thought about it, to do so might have seemed to him to run the risk of superficiality. More importantly, Christian tenets and therefore the life of Christ pervade his whole work, as we shall see.

In a brief late play ironically titled *The Hero*,[11] he uses the metaphor of invisibility to explore "heroism." Mother and Father are sitting separately in a room, she at a table poring over a photograph album, he sitting in a chair reading a magazine. Dressed in a dilapidated blood-stained uniform the dead son enters, but throughout the play he is not visible to his parents. Mother speaks fondly of her dead son, but it becomes clear that neither parent knew of his real life, that both believe, "If it wasn't for the Communists he'd still be alive." Theirs is the conventional view of pragmatic Communism as seen in the West. The son's view is different. His life had been dominated by the pain of being the son of his parents, those paragons who set such store on cleanliness, on proper marriage, on "settling down," and on not questioning the scheme of

A Cell of Good Living

things. Now, after death, he tells them: "Just at the minute I died, one thing was clear in my head. . . . God is a Communist! Either he's down there underneath the mud, underneath the shit, or else He's a bastard! Either he doesn't give bugger, or else He's part of it — and if He's part of it then He has to be a Communist." What Baxter is concerned with here is not any kind of doctrinaire creed or existing political mechanism. What the son had discovered is the deep necessity of *community*, what he had perceived in his instant of awakening was that, in order to be genuine, God must be immersed in the community, in community. Presumably the invisibility works in more than one way. God may be invisible, but He *must* be present. Yet invisibility, the fact that almost no one can see him for what he is, is the central tragedy of Baxter's hero, or rather it is the tragedy of the society in which the hero lives but goes unseen and unacknowledged. In this small play the hero has "returned," though he has changed beyond recognition. He has perceived the true nature of human need, and this, not what would be commonly recognized as any "positive" achievement, is what makes him heroic.

CHAPTER 7

The Virgin and the Witch

It is not wise even for saints to make war on the goddess Venus, or on one or other of her minor representatives. She is seldom reputable. She does not explain herself. One knows that her other face is a skull. Yet without her, the crops fail, beauty goes into mourning and the arts decay.[1]

We are such creatures that we require constant miracles to keep our souls in a state of health. It is Mary who performs for us these hidden miracles of grace.[2]

> Our loves have tied us to the wheel
> From which it is death to be unbound,
> Yet unexpected, unpredictable,
> Like speckled rain that falls on a wave,
> Come the light fingers on the wound,
> Or where the marae meets the cattle hill
> The face of Beatrice moving in the grove.
> (PIL, 15)

JUST as Baxter distinguished between natural man and bourgeois man, he perceived a comparable division in woman. The line of division is not as clear, however. Part is expressed in his explication of "Henley Pub," "The Virgin and the Temptress" (MH, 65 - 89); but in addition to his seeming antithesis between Venus (or Delilah) and Mary, there are traces of the idealized Beatrice and her antithesis, living metamorphoses of the "kitchen god."

Always a fine poet of the sensuous, in a number of poems Baxter celebrates sexual love as "the timelost season of perpetual summer":

> Your mouth was the sun
> And green earth under
> The rose of your body flowering
> Asking and tender
> (BWF, 45)

The Virgin and the Witch

This moment in *Blow, Wind of Fruitfulness* marks the appearance of sexual love as a theme in his work. Early pieces such as the first "Letter to Noel Ginn" and "Haast Pass" express a honey-gathering instinct for "the loves like garden flowers," but perhaps it is no accident that in "The Track" (immediately following "Haast Pass") a tenderly implied early sexual encounter is presided over by Minerva, in her guise as cloud goddess, and it is only after the lovers rise from the crushed ferns that there appears "a glint of blue from the east." The ensuing "Tunnel Beach" somewhat enigmatically portrays the lovers dwarfed by the elemental setting, haunted perhaps by those Furies which were so to beset the life of the young Baxter, with Minerva still poised for vengeance:

> The waist high sea was rolling
> Thunder along her seven iron beaches
> When we climbed down to rocks and the curved sand,
> Drowned Lyonesse lay lost and tolling
> Waiting the cry of the sun's phoenix
> From the sea carved cliffs that held us in their hand.
>
> Forgotten there the green
> Paddocks we walked an hour before,
> The mare and the foal and the witch tormented wood
> And the flaked salt boughs, for the boughs of flame were seen
> Of the first garden and the root
> Of graves in your salt mouth and the forehead branded fire.
>
> Through the rock runnel whined
> The wind, Time's hound in leash,
> And stirred the sand and murmured in your hair,
> The honey of your moving thighs
> Drew down the cirrus sky, your doves about the beach
> Shut out sea thunder with their wings and stilled the lonely air.
>
> But O rising I heard the loud
> Voice of the sea's women riding
> All storm to come. No virgin mother bore
> My heart wave eaten. From the womb of cloud
> Falls now no dove, but combers grinding
> Break sullen on the last inviolate shore.
>   (BWF, 48)

Too raddled with stock responses, caught up in its own rhetoric, "Tunnel Beach" is not a good poem, but it contains two things of interest: the attendance of both virgin and witch and the strong possibility that the poem's real lament is not lost innocence but *non consummatum est*. An earlier piece, "What Shall We Seek For" (BP, 28) appears to suggest sexual love as a means of attaining wholeness. The attitude did not last, but much later, looking back and seeing more clearly, the poet can say:

> The hope of the body was coherent love
> As if the water sighing on the shores
> Would penetrate the hardening muscle, loosen
> Whatever had condemned itself in us
> (PIL, 8)

Belief in the body's truth may lead to vulnerability, to a wound which "heals like a crooked limb / In each of us," but it is preferable to lovelessness; those who suffer the wound are the lucky ones, even though "love grows like the crocus bulb in winter / Hiding from snow and from itself the tender / Green frond in embryo; but dies as rockets die" (FH, 22). Human love is transient, a manifest of "man's heart, that blind Rosetta stone, / Mad as the polar moon, decipherable by none." At worst it is a Pavlovian reflex, or a means of being crushed to death:

> Either this
> Habitual grief whose measured weights grind us,
>
> Or else two Arab lovers chin to chin
> Sewn up in a tightening camel skin
> (*Yearbook* [1964,] 48)

This last, as Baxter later noted, was the "kitchen god's" response to sexual love (MH, 73). A large measure of the grief of human love is attributable to the kitchen god. Baxter continued pessimistic about it:

> ... one may think of tentacles
> Reaching, searching from under the darkest ledge
> And not want to be married.
> To mate with a woman is the choice
> Containing all other kinds of death —
> Fire, water, rock and the airy succubus,
> Without parable, without consolation
> Except that each is the other's boulder and victim.[3]

The Virgin and the Witch

Alongside this sort of thing, for much of the time Baxter took the traditional romantic view of erotic love as opiate (see, for example, the early "Lie Deep, My Love": "Yet in my touch forget all fears" [BWF, 13]). This and other stock tropes of the period show an immature Baxter, whose self-image as "suffering poet" is not yet backed by much experience. Fifteen years later, in such a poem as "Rotorua," desire is seen as rooted in suffering, and this time the knowledge is true:

> Where golden girl and tousled boy
>
> On creaking campbeds tabernacled
> Repeat, repeat the act of kind
>
> As if to the bone flute of Tutanekai.
> Their eyes control the dying summer,
>
> But I am friendlier with those Puritans,
> The dead who rot in single beds
>
> Of concrete where the steam-vents rise,
> Beyond misapprehension, drugs, and those
>
> Demons of lucre and great boredom
> The living cannot exorcise
>
> (*Yearbook* [1961-62] 22)

Perhaps death is better than illusion and suffering; but in some moods Baxter continued to see erotic love as a protective talisman, though by the mid-1960s a sense of love as opiate has given way to acceptance of day-to-day reality, with sexual love as part of it (as in "The Beach House"; PIL, 22). In the new mood of realism which shaped his work from that period on, he looks back upon the adolescent romanticism of unattainable-ideal-loved-one with a certain irony which interpenetrates the agony of his recollected younger self:

> I thought of my Med. Student girlfriend
> Dreaming of horses, cantering brown-eyed horses,
> In her unreachable bed, wrapped in a yellow quilt,
> And something bust inside me. . . .
>
> (PIL, 29, "The Cold Hub")

The horses and the yellow quilt are likely enough reportage, and the well-known fixations of many young riding-school bourgeoises, together with the implications of his own name for natural man, "Horse," will not have escaped Baxter's attention.

In another *Pig Island Letters* poem, "The Harlot" (p. 30), a different kind of subtlety is offered. The Harlot is, in fact, a product of "the moment of art," a sculpted figure above a doorway at Chartres or Rheims Cathedral, but the description of it is evocative of the beauties of the flesh:

> Naked and beautiful, a very human beauty
> And therefore a beauty whose meaning is pity,
> Carried shoulder-high
> By the hawk-headed demons.
>
> The long hair, the face tilted up to the sky
> As if waiting for rain to fall,
> The breasts, the bone cage of the ribs,
> The soft pouch of generation,
> The collarbone — yes, the collarbone in particular. . . .

Enigmatic, the poem's conclusion ("I thought you might be here, she said, / And smiled the broad smile I had seen before") suggests an encounter with the smile of the Mona Lisa, one who knows earth's secrets, with the instant in which Magdalen becomes one with the Virgin. Such a moment complements the sense of natural man in "Tomcat" (PIL, 42), which concludes: "They said / 'Get him doctored.' I think not." Yet elsewhere sex is the focus of guilt, the token of *nada* ("One landscape, many women: / Ambition of that savage empty boy/Haunting the bathing sheds...") and the "Boathouses on the edge of Nowhere" (*Yearbook* [1960], 27).

Of interest in this context is a brief essay in *The Flowering Cross*, "Why Shouldn't Our Priests Marry?" Baxter takes the traditional view, based on the conviction that God's grace is sufficient to compensate for all the inadequacies of this life, that priests should remain celibate. Reinforcing this is awareness of the "emancipation" of women, and that the Church doctrine that a wife should obey her husband has now dropped largely out of practice, so consequently an *animus*-motivated woman might well usurp some of her husband's priestly functions and create a human barrier between him and the members of his flock. Sexual love, therefore, in some circumstances (possibly wider than those of the priestly function) may act as a

The Virgin and the Witch

barrier to a broader and deeper sense of human love. Baxter was of course conscious of the asceticism of the church fathers (and in some moods approved of it), and he must have been aware of the ascetic drive in the early church toward continent marriage, in the lives and preachings of St. Jerome and others. From firsthand experience, too, he would have realized the force of sexual preoccupation as an impediment to the spiritual life.

I The Virgin and the Temptress

Baxter's whole view of woman was traditionalist. Sometimes Pauline, more often he held the Augustinian attitude that, "Through a woman we were sent to destruction; through a woman salvation was sent to us." This antithesis, or paradoxical conjunction, of "Deadeye Adam's lass" and "*Dei Genetrix* / goddess prefigured by / Isis and Semele / thou who dost bruise under thy heel the serpent," occurs in his work as early as *Traveller's Litany*, and the poem chosen to give the title to his volume of selected poems, *The Rock Woman*, a piece first published in the 1955 *Poetry Yearbook*, concludes:

> Magdalen of the rock
> Unvirgin pray for us.
> In the wave's throb our agonies awake
> Rise to your true all-suffering kiss.
> You ask for us the death-hour's peace.
> (RW, 27)

"Wave's throb" here is a figure for human life, the sea of Chaos, in which the weak and defeated become the drowned, as in "At Taieri Mouth" or "Fishermen." Fear of drowning, temptation by it, runs all the way through the traveler's soliloquy of "Henley Pub" (MH, 88 - 89), which Baxter elaborates on in "The Virgin and the Temptress" (MH). Here the witch-figure is Delilah, one guise of woman, calculating and altogether heartless; but Baxter points out that the puritan nay-sayer in man would regard even the Dusseldorf Venus, the big-hipped mother of civilization, as a whore.

II *Mother*

Of "Henley Pub" he says: "My hero is a man who has not traveled far from the gates of the womb; hence, his extreme vulnerability to the faults of the flesh. There is an undeveloped Oedipal quality in his relation to his mistress, in his closeness to water and earth, in the complete passivity of his Marian devotion. Women are all mothers to him" (MH, 75). In the previous chapter, thinking about Baxter's "hero" or protagonist, I found it difficult to decide whether to include Oedipus or not. His treatment of Oedipus and the Oedipus complex is perhaps the point where Baxter, in C. K. Stead's opinion, suffuses his work "with the charge of a particular emotion which belongs to the poet rather than to something he has observed in the world beyond himself."[4] Stead's point is somewhat obscure. Apparently he subscribed, when he wrote it, to T. S. Eliot's dictum that good poetry is dependent on the separation of sufferer from creator, or to Allen Curnow's assertion that there must be "a reality prior to the poem" (by which he meant, external to the poet); but such views are relative, not absolute. We may admit, without negative implication, that there is a subjective, expressionist drive in much of Baxter's work. The question is: to what extent did he see Oedipal qualities as decisive in the life of modern Western man?

Regrettably, a definitive answer is not available, but we can trace an Oedipal element through his work. An early example is connected with the manuscript fair copy of "The Mountains." Alongside the poem in the notebook is written, "Mountains are mothers," while in the poem itself a refrain line, "The mountains crouch like tigers," is amplified by portrayal of "Men shut within a whelming bowl of hills" (BP,9). A little later death itself is equated with "The wild lost city of a mother's love" (BWF, 21), and then in "The Homecoming" (PU, 21), "grief's Penelope" is the mother of Odysseus the traveler, and the old covenant to which he returns is dominated by his mother. Much later, in "Waipatiki Beach" (PIL, 25), the "oldest Venus. . . . / The manifold mother" is identified with: "Her lion face, the skull-brown Hekate / Ruling my blood since I was born." Here the mother is equated with dark forces, the face of evil, with Hekate, who may also be Proserpine, mistress of the underworld, representative of moonless darkness, or, as in the poem, "that female ghost, the daylight moon." Writing of Burns' "Tam O' Shanter," Baxter refers to "the *anima,* that mysterious archetype who has been called variously Venus, Cybele, Artemis . . . Hekate, patroness of witches, the goddess of the underworld" (MH, 116). Later he says that the *anima* "represents . . . all that is not-self. She cannot be constructed; she has to be discovered." Again we are dealing in somewhat obscure materials, particularly since earlier in this same essay, Baxter has made the very *horse* female: "The man's strength lies in his horse — it is she who joins him to the earth, she who

The Virgin and the Witch

carries him out of danger, she who suffers mutilation because of his rashness. The man is male, the horse female, signifying an active and a passive principle. I think the grey mare symbolizes the personal subconscious in its entirety, seen as a protective and maternal power belonging to the earth . . . "(MH, 108). Highly intuitive, somewhat of a jumble, this conglomeration of ideas suggests that for Baxter both the not-self and the subconscious were female, the first both beguiling and threatening, the second "protective and maternal," both merging in the projected mother-figures of his poems. This digression on the mother, however, would be incomplete were we not to note that the human mother-figure eventually gives way to Gea, the Earth Mother, in whom are the source and order of creation.

III Virgin

Part of this field of intuition and feeling is Baxter's devotion to Mary, Mother of God. His little essay "The Spirit of Mary" (*The Flowering Cross*, 12 - 16) warns against the setting up of a dualism involving Mary, as representative of the virtue of all that belongs to oneself, as against what is unfamiliar and therefore malign. Rather, he declares, Mary is "the foremost member of the Church Triumphant," and (following Thomas Merton) our knowledge of Her helps to lift our sense of Christ from abstraction to humanity. She is mother of "All who howl in the rusty frying pan" (HB, 56) of human existence.

The traveling salesman of "Henley Pub" (MH, 88 - 89) invokes Mary's help to overcome the death of God in him and the onset of suicidal despair, the occasion of which is Delilah. The river of life has become "the bog-black stream" of the Styx. Certainly not one of Baxter's magnificent best, the poem reveals a good deal of his inner landscape. Of his protagonist he comments: "His life has become polarized between the Blessed Virgin, an archetype of the good mother, and the Temptress, an archetype of the bad mother, with the dubious implication that the first rules over the spirit, the second over the flesh" (MH, 78). He takes care to say that for him Mary is "an historical person." Not an idealization, she is, on the contrary, representative of the grace possible in everyday human existence. Such grace is available in human sexuality. Devoted, like Stephen Dedalus, to the being whom James Joyce calls "B.V.M.," Baxter was yet fascinated by an earthier sense of woman, and, as O'Sullivan astutely attests, in "Henley Pub" the "holy Queen" "is not the match Baxter believes her to be for that malign Venus."[5]

"Pig Island Letters" runs a gamut of female "archetypes," from "That brisk gaunt woman in the kitchen" through "I made a mother of the keg," and the idealized "face of Beatrice moving in the grove," to the closing section, which is a dialogue with Mary at the Gate of Heaven (a moment complementary to her vigil at the foot of the cross, or, following O'Sullivan's suggestion, Demeter's "awaiting her lost child at the gate of Hades"). In this dialogue Mary asks questions but passes no judgment. Even though the answers to her questions are negative and the Supplicant is unwashed, thirsting, and has lost the precious jewel she gave into his safekeeping, she allows him to enter into the gate, for she is the fount of mercy, the means by which a sinner may find his way back to the lost green garden. In the phrase of Baxter's translation from Rimbaud, "The First Communions" (RW, 73), she proffers "ice-crystals of pardon."

IV The Temptress

Dead-bright as a corpse
Under the lightning she came,
Mother Carey,
The blind hoor of the sea.
Sh'd eyes like a blowlamp, captain,
Lips like a bomb shelter,
Sharks in her natural quarter
And a necklace of drowned men's jawbones.
(Traveller's Litany)

Baxter's poetry does not display a schematized cast of characters, each playing a distinctive role. The temptress figure, examined in detail in "The Virgin and the Temptress," can shift from a figure of predatory sexuality to being Queen of Death, and the latter itself shifts in value in the course of Baxter's career from being a figure of dread to being a figure of welcome. Let us return, for the moment, to Delilah in "Henley Pub," representative of female sexual power, possessing "the honorary status of a queen," chaining her lover to her by the witchcraft of her body. Once alluring and enticing, she has become witchlike and threatening: "The terrible phase in any liaison is the point where the subconscious projections with which each partner has been willing to clothe the other cease to be positive; when the figure of the beloved changes from life-giver, consoler, perfect friend and mirror, to something else — vampire, living corpse, Jack the Ripper, spider woman, werewolf. It is the negative side of the romantic equation, firmly repressed at the beginning of the

The Virgin and the Witch

liaison but likely to come to the surface as it proceeds" (MH, 81). As a perceptive study of this phenomenon, he instances Doris Lessing's *The Golden Notebook*. Noteworthy is the point that the dreadful change is not altogether a transformation but rather a revelation of forces already present, the potentiality of death. Later in his explanation of "Henley Pub," Baxter describes Delilah as "corpse-like," "a living corpse," and this state is equated, somewhat later again, with lovelessness. "Letter to the World," a powerful poem of the mid-1950s, is apposite here:

> Salt wife, when you were pregnant with your death
> You asked me for the kiss of a kind mirror
> And newly married then I knew no better.
> I praised you for the paint upon your scabs
> And left out evil from each loving letter.
> Now as the serpent stabs
> Of grief in my guts, among the wounds and swabs
> Of love's rough hospital to your proud flesh I come
> And the soul sweating in its iron lung.
> (IFN, 52)

In *Pig Island Letters* he has the same range of experience in mind when he writes of the local women:

> A skinny wench in jeans with a kea's eye:
> The rack on which our modern martyrs die.
>
> I prophesy these young delinquent bags
> Will graduate to grim demanding hags.
> (p. 6)

One of the poems in the 1964 *Poetry Yearbook* which caused Baxter's altercation with the State Literary Fund is "The Girl in Yellow Jeans," which begins as an account of a travesty of "Love," the small fountain of Eros, and ends at the instant of the girl's discovering the vampire in herself. This vampire element is close to the capacity to use other people with indifference, without a sense of their humanity, and its seed is in the very nature of human relationships, as is shown, say, in "The Surfman's Story" (PU, 14), in which a woman swimmer who has made a suicide pact to drown with her lover, is rescued and later marries her surfman-rescuer.

The Rock Woman includes a fair sprinkling of "temptress" poems. Among them, besides "Henley Pub," are pieces such as

"The Harlot" and "Thoughts of a Remuera Housewife." Reminiscent of a figure from *The Waste Land*, feeding on tranquillizers, this last, an overtly bourgeois woman, sees herself inwardly as queen of the Underworld, "mad, happy, lost!" in promiscuity; she is a Proserpine, both temptress and sufferer.

"Henley Pub" and "Thoughts of a Remuera Housewife" are typical instances of Baxter's connecting sex and despair, but perhaps his extreme example of the cruelty brought about by man's sexual appetite is the Japanese girl Eioko (HB, 28) who is reduced to "an aching cistern," an instance of what O'Sullivan calls "the dramatic figures who carry Baxter's approbation, in that expanding situation where God's love seems to be in direct proportion to physical distress and social anathema." "Eioko" is a clear contrasting of Eros and caritas, and incidentally reveals man's own projection of the temptress. Eioko herself is a martyr, sold into slavery by her father Choshi, displayed like a carcass, offered up for the pleasure of "Tourist, soldier, ape and boor," but finally sharing her rice bowl with those poorer than herself. Emphasized here is the reduction of a human being to an object in the interests of commerce and erotic satisfaction. Some element in man welcomes the vampire, then barters for its favors, and finally reduces it to this "butcher's meat." On the other hand, in "Divorcee" in *The Lion Skin*, the woman ponders:

> Better any man
> Than the red hot pike of solitude
> Thrusting and twisting — but the only ceiling
> I ever really liked was that
>
> First one, the brown high slats of the boathouse
> On my first honeymoon. . . .

The demon Custom has got hold of her, but left her with a vestige of the instinct for human contact. Another poem in *The Lion Skin*, "Husband," which begins in a life-denying tone, is one of the most positive in all of Baxter's work, a momentary transformation of the temptress. The protagonist is looking at his wife, moving slowly in the kitchen, arranging a bowl of japonica:

> To my eroded
> Sight she resembled the earth itself, the long-haired
> Daughter of Zeus who likes whatever happens
> Because it happens to her.

V The Kitchen God

Wives, in Baxter's world, are not usually so accepting or complaisant. Most often they are in the grip of "the kitchen god," the terrible pseudodeity which transforms sexual love into something far less attractive. The kitchen god is "the crude, unshaped conscience of the tribe" (MH, 73). Preeminently a god of safety, he tempts man away from self-knowledge to retreat into childhood pieties; thus he is a prime source of schizophrenia. Enemy of Priapus, it is he who insists upon fig leaves on nude statues. He abhors Dionysus and is at all-out war with Apollo, the god of art. Since the kitchen god is a principle of order, Baxter, in the context of his discussion of "Henley Pub," professes not to disapprove entirely; but in general he is an active enemy of the kitchen god's repression and sees that repression as crucial in striking the balance between human love and human society, since, in melancholy practice, these two cannot be one and the same.

Accepted morality, particularly with regard to sex and when it chooses to ignore the specific circumstances of individuals, is the chief manifestation of the kitchen god; this is the framework of the early sequence "Cressida," and the basis of an early short story, "To Have and to Hold" (*Numbers*, no. 5), which contains a virtually complete account of the antagonism between natural man and the kitchen god. The young wife (the characters are not given names) is shown in her ordered kitchen, arranging flowers (irises, on this occasion). Approached by her husband, she has an anxious air which is familiar to him. His inner vision of her (his sexual fantasy) is of a wild Scythian mare, his outer contact is with a totally inaccessible woman. Together, once, they had envisioned their prospective marriage: a beach house, their making kelp bags in which to gather mussels, their idly skipping stones over the waves. But in his eyes she has proved repressive, rationing sexual encounter, ordering her life around their child. He, in response, has taken refuge in drink and reminiscences. Yet, on their anniversary, on impulse he buys her a red rose; but when he might go home to her he is waylaid by the thought of a comforting beer. Rose and beer together bring back his vision of the "Wild mare of Scythia, fertilised by the wind"; he returns home eventually, to find that she has prepared an orderly feast. Her frown has deepened, and they quarrel because of his unpunctuality and the forbidden beer.

The very banality of detail in this story heightens its effect. We momentarily overlook the fact that it is *his* version of the situation.

At any rate it shows the ever-present antagonism between the kitchen god and the desire in man for an uninhibited freedom. Such appeared to be Baxter's view of things for most of his life, but at least once, in "The Flowering Cross," he was careful to distinguish between a proper freedom and license: "I have no quarrel with the existence of sexual love in the world. Indeed, most of the poetry or prose or plays I have written include it freely as one of the liveliest factors in human growth. But a view of marriage which gives an absolute priority to sexual love, and either ignores or demotes to second place the love that is actually a form of mercy, can only lead to the break-up of a great number of marriages; for sexual love belongs to the subconscious mind, that arena of dreams and myths and magical suppositions . . ." (FC, 93). Many people may see such statements as untypical of Baxter, who almost invariably seemed to perceive in the derelict and sinful a source of hidden strength, but another and less flamboyant Baxter characteristic was respect for moral rigor in human relations.

In terms of New Zealand society, the figurehead for the kitchen god is Queen Victoria, a sort of pseudo-Mary, who has left for inheritance "the bone acre / of your cages and laws," the land of suburbia in which the man returns home to his wife from the office by train, among the office girls, who "for once are flaring / Crocuses in the town's grey jungle." "Safe home he looks / At her kitchen face, and knows his luck is out" (*Yearbook* [1964], 47).

The early sections which set the scene, of "Pig Island Letters" are haunted by the kitchen god:

> Wives in the kitchen cease to smile as we go
> Into the gap itself, the solid night
> Where poor drunks fear the icy firmament:
> (PIL, 3)

In Section 2 the wife is portrayed as

> That brisk gaunt woman in the kitchen
> Feeding the coal range, sullen
> To all strangers lest one should be
> Her antique horn-red Satan.

Section 4 claims that "Our women chiefly carry in their bones / The curse that stuck to the scattered oven stones." And section 10 contains the lines:

> To outflank age — a corrugated shack
> With fried pauas in the pan
> Beside a bay somewhere, grandchildren in tribes
> Wrestling in the long grass, seawater, sleep,
> While cloud and green tree like sisters keep
> The last door for the natural man.
>
> It will be what it is, a half-life,
> For the mystery requires
> A victim — Marsyas the manbeast
> Hung up and flayed on a fir tree,
> Or a death by inches, catheter and wife
> Troubling an old man's vanity.

Ultimately, however, his view (expressed in such pieces as the broadsheet "A Small Ode on Mixed Flatting") appears to have been that both man and woman, husband and wife, are equally in the hands of the kitchen god:

> Not that the country is made up of islands
> Or that our women drag like mules
> Us to Utopia by the apron-strings,
> A bach, a fridge, a car,
> But that the mind has lost the earth it rules.[6]

But perhaps the most corrosive anatomizing of the repressive kitchen god is "Ballad of Calvary Street," with its summary portrayal of a long marriage:

> And so these two old fools are left,
> A rosy pair in evening light,
> To question Heaven's dubious gift,
> To hag and grumble, growl and fight:
> The love they kill won't let them rest,
> Two birds that peck in one fouled nest.
>   (HB, 54)

VI *Love Poems*

Venus, Mary, Beatrice, and the subversion of these by the kitchen god — this has amounted to a consideration of Baxter's view of woman and her place in the fabric of New Zealand life. Another facet of that view is his love poems, which range from the early and abstract sequence of "Love Lyrics," some of which appear in

Beyond the Palisade, right up to the long title sequence of *Autumn Testament* (1972). Some of these poems, such as "Haast Pass" and "The Track," or "Pyrrha," concern the protagonist's sexual initiation. Others, such as "Let Time Be Still" and "My Love Late Walking" are rather formal celebrations of the loved one and the relationship itself. Three poems in *Howrah Bridge and Other Poems*, "The Apple Tree," "She Who is Like the Moon," and "On the Death of Her Body" (HB, 45 - 47) (which is similar in approach to "My Love Late Walking"), are much more immediate and direct:

> I do not know another beauty
> Like what your face has shown
> Silently, silently. . . .

After this opening "She Who is Like the Moon" descends to stock response, but the strongest of the three, "On the Death of Her Body," sustains a much greater degree of felt life, perhaps because it is also a projection of the fear of oblivion.

Baxter's earliest love poems are examples of a generalized, disembodied romanticism, which persisted in his work through the 1960s. Yet an important implication even in the earliest work is that sexual love may give a meaning to existence. Very often Baxter wrote of love in relation to time, mortality, eternity, in some instances (such as "Let Time Be Still" and "Tunnel Beach") suggesting that the experience of erotic love could stay time's sad erosions. Somewhat later he came to develop the opposite view, that sensual experience is itself part of the process of dying (such is the mood even of the relatively early "Rocket Show"). Reviewing *The Fallen House*, Robert Chapman summarized Baxter's attitudes to love as follows: "we must first love God to make love whole again."[7] With an evergrowing sense of its reality, this was the deepest level of his apperception of love. We shall be looking at religious aspects of Baxter's life and work in chapter nine, but some of Mr. Chapman's points are interesting in the present context. He feels that Baxter coveted, rather than possessed, belief, and that such love is for him "a plan of life" the origins of which are revealed in "To My Father" (FH, 14). Mr. Chapman goes on to suggest that Baxter's stoic resignation derives from a sense of the failure of brotherly love. More immediately relevant, he considers that Baxter felt "we are driven by the force of feeling . . . a crippled form of passion," even though we know that only havoc can come of it. Like Baudelaire,

The Virgin and the Witch

Baxter wants "the personal enjoyment of chaos"; it is this in him which welcomed the embrace of the Witch.

A mood of reveling in chaos may be found also in *The Night Shift* and *In Fires of No Return*. By the time he published *Howrah Bridge* Baxter had come to feel that human love is inseparable from suffering. The autobiographical element of *Pig Island Letters* refers to his early and continuing predilection for erotic experiences, but from this time on he apparently felt in himself a diminishment of such urges. Weir quotes an undated letter from that period: "My own natural desire would be for apples, wine and concubines and loud shouting. But no; very quietly one has to accept the Fall and love the fallen; which means to feel in one's bones the process of detachment from life . . ." (Weir, 40 - 41). A movement toward acceptance of death, this detachment confronts us with a paradox. To the long tradition of regarding sexual encounter itself as a form of dying, Baxter has added a dimension, seeing the Fall as a death:

> In a room where the wind clattered the blind-cord
> In the bed of a girl with long plaits
> I found the point of entry,
> The place where father Adam died.
>
> (PIL, 5)

So, deprivation of sexual activity is itself a form of death, which brings us back to the threefold woman: Mary, Venus, Beatrice. Although Baxter's ultimate devotion was professedly to Mary, we have seen that he recognized the force, the inevitability, and even the positive value of Venus. For full humanity, it seems, both the Baudelairian and Christian levels of love need to be experienced. As he says in "The Flowering Cross," though, it is disastrous to make a "Religion" of erotic love, with "women regarding men as heroes, and men regarding women as goddesses." From it and from our idolatry of affluence, health, and physical beauty, "when sickness, poverty or the loss of good looks enter the marriage circle, our young people may feel subconsciously betrayed. In fact, a new kind of love is being asked of them" (FC, 97). Baxter's full sense of what this means will emerge in our final chapter.

CHAPTER 8

Unveiling Chaos: Baxter's Drama

Without the dramatic role, life tends to be experienced as chaos. The unveiling of this chaos is perhaps the theme of all my plays.[1]

A critical purist could be forgiven for detecting unconscious irony in this remark of Baxter's, for none of his plays has formal distinction. Of the twenty-odd he wrote (listed in the Appendix) few, if any, are as accomplished as his best poetry. While the twentieth century has seen solid development in New Zealand poetry and fiction, there are still very few plays of any note. As Baxter said in his introduction to *The Devil and Mr Mulcahy*, he felt himself to be in territory with "large areas of unbroken ground waiting for the plough and the spade";[2] thus he saw himself as a pioneer, but adds with careful modesty, "without an inspired and sympathetic producer, I would not have written the plays."[3]

Hal Smith, in his useful "Baxter's Theatre: A Critical Appraisal," neatly links these (late) plays to the Jerusalem period, which followed so soon after them: "Baxter's first move into the theatre could be seen as the first phase of the total social involvement of his last years devoted to social criticism and social experimentation in (the) North Island."[4] Written in Baxter's Burns Fellowship years, the plays produced by Patric Carey at the Globe in Dunedin were by no means a "first move." That had come more than a decade earlier, with publication of "Jack Winter's Dream" in the September 1956 issue of *Landfall*.

Six plays have now been published in book form, a few others are available in acting copies, one or two as theater programs. Some scripts are unobtainable. A complete account of Baxter's drama is not at present possible, and little purpose would be served in taking each accessible play and explicating it in terms of plot, character, and the Aristotelian unities. From what evidence there is we can draw working conclusions about Baxter's capabilities as a playwright and see how his drama relates to his work generally.

Reviewing Richard Campion's Wellington production of Baxter's second play, *The Wide Open Cage* (1959), and seeing in it "a sort of New Zealand *Lower Depths*," James Bertram offers a succinct summary of observations Baxter made to a postperformance discussion group: "He said that his central purpose was psychological, that he had intended to present compulsive characters acting compulsively; that he preferred Strindberg to O'Casey; and that Aristotle was out of date."[5] Baxter responded in a quatrain which seems to put the classical rules for drama in league with New Zealand's lowering secular puritanism:

> When Skully trod upon the stage
> Mrs Grundy groaned with rage.
> Upend her, boys! And then we'll throttle
> The old grey ghost of Aristotle.

Ever willing to rout the tenacious Mrs. Grundy, he changed his mind eventually about Aristotle (apparently with some guidance from Professor H. D. F. Kitto, the noted classical scholar, who was visiting at Otago when Baxter was Burns Fellow); but the shift, according to his explanation of it in a lecture, was toward subjectivity: unity of action means "a coherent myth" expressed in terms of local knowledge and experience; unity of time is the lifespan, the "permanent now" of Everyman; unity of place is the stage itself, a little universe whereon the members of the audience project "the communal drama of their own minds." By no means a faithful interpretation of the Aristotelian unities, these definitions offer useful enough guidelines to Baxter's drama.

Very often one has the impression that it is he, the playwright, who is the "projector." The focusing consciousness of his first play, *Jack Winter's Dream*, is an externalized counterpart of himself in the form of a narrator, a mechanism which first came to his attention in Laurie Lee's radio play *Magellan*,[6] but which he developed along lines established by Dylan Thomas in *Under Milkwood*. Thomas' influence combined with that of Synge to produce a Baxter variant of pseudo-Celtic prose-poetry, supposed to have derived from the Scots dialect of Otago and the Southern Lakes (specifically, near Naseby), and based too on "fertile conversations" with Archibald Baxter, "on every subject from alluvial gold mining to demonology."[7]

Over the years, the use of language in drama continued to be a preoccupation of Baxter's. "If it is the language of the people it is figurative language," he said when the *New Zealand Listener* interviewed him about *Jack Winter's Dream*. Synge could draw on such language, "But you cannot do that here." Instead he manufactured a "poetic" idiom which would no doubt be equally breathless on Aran, in darkest Swansea or rockbound in Cromwell Gorge:

Who is singing on the night road when only the scared owls can hear him? It is Jack Winter, swagman and station rouseabout. Sixty-eight convictions for being happy in a public place. . . . Twin brother to the Ephesian sleepers, he has forgotten the world of manhours and ordered mischief, wishes, agonies, hot love and cold pillows, plaster gnomes and paper doilies, for a lifelong dream in which he is winter walking Adam, and the green, gay, hole-and-corner, rabbit-footed, duck-blooded, river-voiced, bush-thighed and mountain-breasted earth his care and his sole kingdom.

To quote this, naked as it were, is not entirely fair. Baxter himself had a highly cultivated, mannered voice-production; yet (although he never succeeded in creating fully authentic stage dialogue) few New Zealanders can have been more conscious of the colloquial speech of their countrymen. Of a piece with his own involvements, he was particularly aware of the idiom of what he sometimes called "pub conversation." He regarded language as he regarded Western man (and woman), in dualistic terms: on the one hand, "the deadpan banalities of our bureaucracies (invaluable for satiric use)," on the other, the language of the street or public house. By the time he wrote *The Band Rotunda* (1967) he had a clearer sense of "the vigour of street language" and how to employ his boasted "unlimited reservoir of biological metaphors and existential anecdotes."[8] What he was after was truth to local detail plus concreteness and particularity, as is evident from his example, the drinker in the iron foundry who raised his glass and said: "The men up in the marble orchard would like to have a bit of this." In writing dialogue Baxter seemed to feel easiest with an idiom which was basically proletarian, but heightened by a rich sense of poetry. Another source transfusing his speakers' words is what he calls "Biblical prose-poetry," a component of *The Devil and Mr Mulcahy*, which nonetheless seems a thinner-textured play than *The Band Rotunda*.

Character contrast between Oedipus and Theseus in *The Temptations of Oedipus* (probably written in 1968) is provided largely by differing resonances of language, though this is as much a matter of the phenomenology of the play as a whole as it is of the idiom solely. Theseus discourses almost invariably of the surface (as befits one whose chief concern is with the things of this world, controlling them); Oedipus speaks more metaphorically and apocalyptically, in a manner befitting a fallen and destitute monarch. O. E. Middleton sensitively observes that the "recurrence of images identifying water and wine with blood, bread with rotting flesh, the sun with an ulcer, give rise to curiously ironical and dissonant echoes and reverberations in the mind when the words are used or suggested in their more usual connotation (as Antigone invites her father to eat bread and meat after a long speech; or when King Theseus says to Cleomenes: 'You will live to kiss your wife and bake another batch...'").[9] Oedipus' characteristic language is a mere patina if we evaluate experience as Theseus does. Baxter's whole career makes evident that he does not. As a young writer he was ridden and carried away by rhetoric, but in these late works, at his best, he has more control over the functional use of language. In *The Temptations of Oedipus*, words, language, have become a theme. Double irony lurks in Theseus' remark that "without words, what happens is never," and his instant arrest of the citizen who words him: "Kings do not go hungry!" Nor do they let pass such calorie-laden accusations, without devouring the speaker.

I Technique

Being now aware of Baxter's attitude to Aristotle, and his sense of the importance of language in theater, we should take a broader look at his dramatic techniques. Probably because of the virtual nonexistence of New Zealand theater in the 1950s, his first play was a radio play, and this demanded a specific approach. He told the *Listener*, "In a radio play ... all those things that would otherwise, on the stage, be visual — gesture, setting and appearance of actors — must find emotional equivalents in the spoken word. That is why the poetic prose method is very suitable." Obviously, it was innately Baxter's notion that the equivalent had to be "emotional." Hence developed what Howard McNaughton describes as Baxter's "expressionist" radio plays.[10] Perhaps taking a hint from James Bertram, McNaughton states a strong case for Strindberg's "dream plays" as an important source of Baxter's impressionism (and, remember, there is Barry Humphries' epigram about New Zealand: "a play by Strindberg with music by Mantovani"). Baxter was well aware of the subjectivity of his plays, the likelihood that many of his characters emerged, horned or hornless, from what he once called his "menagerie of interior selves." Once when acting the part of the doctor in Chekhov's *Three Sisters* he discovered that the actor, too, must dig into himself to discover that area of his consciousness corresponding to the character he is attempting to play. Baxter's overall sense of the drama, then, was highly subjective, for he believed that the participation of actors, playwright, and audience, all three, is subjective.

Jack Winter's Dream is an obvious projection. McNaughton says that in a "dream play" there should be some kind of a "distorting agent to act as a lens" (185). Often in the most powerful of Baxter's scenes two elements in particular serve to heighten the action (or "distort," or give apocalyptic overtones to it). One is the destitution brought about by alcohol or betrayal or lost love; the other is the "abyss" of mortality, together with the big question about God's nature and its effect on individuals' lives (probably these sorts of concerns led Baxter to think of his plays as "psychological").

A repeated Baxter technique is the staging of scenes combining (or paralleling) "live" and "dead" characters. His own list of themes in *Jack Winter's Dream* reads: "Age in the person of Jack Winter; death, in the murder of the young miner; and love — in the scene between the young miner and the pub-keepers's daughter." Death, in fact, is the framework of the piece, for Webfoot Charlie and the others at the Drover's Rest are all dead. Charlie's murder of the young Trevelyan, who feels the stirrings of love for the daughter Jenny, is a death within a death. Preacher Lowry, in the closing scene, touches upon Webfoot Charlie's lack of conscience, the "distorting agent" which results in his murdering his own natural successor. Webfoot's lack gives him the devil's pride and a curious kind of freedom, except perhaps from his bone-handled razor, still a potent and expressive image, the more so since it is beyond the grave.

Baxter uses the dream in two later radio plays and in both makes some use of passing through the gap between life and death. Unhappy in the present, the protagonist of *The First Wife* (1966) daydreams about past associations and encounters his Younger Self, a Sea Woman (who is also Lilith) and an Ancestor. This is one of those plays in which Baxter (as McNaughton puts it) "found an outlet for private myths and personae which had been accumulating since boyhood." *Mr Brandywine Chooses a Gravestone* (1966) concerns the imminent death of the eponymous character, and his isolation and consequent turning in upon himself (the theme, in fact, of Tolstoy's "The Death of Ivan Ilyich"). Flashback, nostalgia, reminiscence and dream are the play's means, and Brandywine, in colloquy with the dead, is put to exploring how to confront his own death. A play discussed briefly in chapter 6 above, *The Hero*, features a dead soldier eavesdropping on his parents, who reminisce about him and ponder war and the external causes of his death.

All that has been said thus far may suggest some weaknesses of Baxter's technique. One is a tendency (confined largely, but not entirely, to the earlier plays) toward "poeticality"; another is a fault attributable to his central view of literature, that it affects men's conduct, or ideally should do so — he is at times inclined to be discursive. A countervailing tendency is for the action, at times, to be perfunctory.

Such points bring us to the general question of form. We have seen a little of what Baxter felt about Aristotle. Nonetheless he was very conscious of the problems of form in the theater. One danger he saw in his own work was the tendency to make his characters mere mouthpieces for his own views. For example, he felt that the doctrinaire priest in *The Wide Open Cage* stalled the play with his set pieces about the relation of God to man and man to his neighbor. One attempt to overcome this was *The Spots on the Leopard* (1962), badly panned in New York and full of gimmickry like a students' capping show.

The Spots on the Leopard was a temporary, if not altogether untypical, aberration. Centerless chaos was not an important attribute of Baxter's best plays. Rather it was a kind of static quality (the "permanent now"!) endemic to a drama of projected ideas, feelings, and images. For all that he claimed — and he did so more than once — that his drama was "psychological," it was not (except in some cases in the Americanized sense in which O'Neill's drama may be described as "psychological," i. e., because it deals with the compulsive). Nowhere is character development or character exploration important. That is not what Baxter is concerned with, even though, it seems, he mistakenly thought so. He realized, of course, that initially he had given his characters set pieces to deliver (each reciting his poem in turn, as it were), but he came to perceive that "the total play resembled the total poem," or, as he put it in the introduction to *The Sore-Footed Man*, a play is "a metaphoric structure in which the multiple statements of the characters correspond to the accumulated images of a poem."[11] Just as earlier the phrase about "emotional equivalent" seems to limit him to a certain approach in radio plays, so here the words "metaphoric structure" are, as Hal Smith notices, a commitment and a limitation. Smith makes a parallel between Baxter's drama and the poetic drama of Lorca, suggesting that both sacrifice possible psychological depth in their characters to the use of characters as symbols. In this respect, the strength Baxter's poetry undoubtedly gained from his mythologizing and from a life-giving consciousness of the "mythical substratum" available in Greek myths and legends proves to be a weakness in the plays, for it leads to a predetermined (and consequently static) structure.

An attendant weakness in those plays where Baxter kept to the original Greek setting is occasional use of anachronistic language, mixing modern idiom with language necessarily directly "translated." On the other hand, the plays given "modern" settings (*The Bureaucrat* and *Mr O'Dwyer's Dancing Party*) suffer a thinness of texture consequent on their updating.

II *Influences*

As was the poet, Baxter the dramatist was "highly syncretic." Having seen how he adapted (or did not quite adapt) Dylan Thomas and was influenced, not altogether syncretically perhaps, by both the theory and practice of Strindberg, let us look briefly at other influences.

J. M. Synge has been mentioned in the same context as Thomas, and indeed to similar effect, as Baxter acknowledged when he was talking about *Jack Winter's Dream*. Another connection sometimes made is with Eugene O'Neill, and there are striking general parallels between Baxter's work and such O'Neill plays as *Desire Under the Elms*, *A Touch of the Poet*, and *A Moon for the Misbegotten*. Quite apart from the fact that they share a predilection for drunken heroes, Baxter and O'Neill each attempted to adapt an original folk idiom into a secondary culture, and in *The Devil and Mr Mulcahy* Baxter offers a sort of Pavlova-cake version of the incest theme so characteristic of O'Neill. He deals with the same theme more coolly in *The Temptations of Oedipus*, where Ismene says of her original seduction by her brother Eteocles, "I felt I was taking the whole tormented world in my arms," thus reminding us of O'Neill's earth-mother heroine in *A Moon for the Misbegotten*. Both women are whores of good heart, and both see that the central human problem is love, which, in Ismene's words, "the gods do not preserve."

Another, and very different, influence is that of Bertolt Brecht, apparently momentary, on *The Starlight in Your Eyes* (1967), which McNaughton describes as "a coherently Brechtian drama . . . didactic . . . propagandist." Brecht would have appealed to Baxter's sense of the drama as a communal enterprise and perhaps also to his pedagogical and moralizing side. Brecht's didacticism of "alienation" (his own term for objectification) finds a counterpart in Baxter's parable-making facility, and Baxter (in a comment which savors of Jacques Ellul) described the German Marxist's plays as "parables of the human condition in which man is inveterately insecure, the builder and abandoner of cities." Perhaps he had in mind Brecht's peasant-judge in *The Caucasian Chalk Circle* when he once posited an imagined drama in which the protagonist asks himself how it is that he is at one and the same time a criminal and not a criminal, for as always Baxter's Manichean man is one puzzled by his own amalgam of innocence and guilt.

Like Brecht, Baxter could make good dramatic use of a variety of poetic forms, particularly ballad (a characteristic he shared also with his near-contemporary Brendan Behan). Again, his tendency toward discursiveness (in say *The Devil and Mr Mulcahy* or *The Sore-Footed Man*, where he is conscious of making dramatic use of what he terms "bureaucratic language") bears a slight resemblance to Brechtian "alienation," but where Brecht was anti-individualist, Baxter was a long way in spirit from attempted distancing and objectivity, so that he sometimes intrudes upon his dramatic characters for reasons quite opposite to Brecht's.

Another brief, and again very different, influence was that of Samuel Beckett. Baxter once said that he saw in the Theatre of the Absurd "evidence of a gigantic spiritual struggle to express the tragedy that occurs when tragedy loses its meaning," as he felt it had when, in Vietnam, the diabolic destruction of hundreds of villages by napalm was controlled from "the glass castle of the bureaucracies." In 1961, "The Silver Plate," Baxter's eclogue in honor of Samuel Beckett, was broadcast. Otherwise the influence is traceable in two short, sparsely existential plays, *The Rendezvous* and *The World Is*, and in three mimes, *The Woman, The Cross*, and *The Axe and the Mirror*. Both slight and unremarkable, the two plays show evidence of Beckett's tone and texture. Of the mimes, Marilyn Parker has provided a sensitive account.[12] Two at least were conceived to accompany full-length plays, *The Woman* to precede *The Sore-Footed Man*, *The Axe and the Mirror* as prelude to *The Bureaucrat*. Presumably *The Cross* accompanied *The Band Rotunda*.

Although Marilyn Parker suggests that the mimes are weaker taken without their accompanying plays, it is noticeable that together they form a kind of thematic sequence. *The Woman* enacts a birth, a discovery of the Woman by the Man born to her, and eventually their mating. *The Axe and the Mirror* concerns a childlike figure who plays with its own reflection in a mirror, is frustrated by loss of the light source, and attempts to break out of confinement with an axe only to have it bounce off the walls. Parker's comment is illuminating: "He discovers his likeness in a mirror, a continuation here, perhaps, of the discovery of like and unlike in *The Woman*, and eventually makes love to his own reflection" (64). Thus the mimes may be said to suggest existential states of isolation, narcissism, and yet partnership and opposites. Completing a possible sequence, *The Cross* deals with death; it contains an "orgasmic self-crucifixion" and a beautiful mask covering a grinning death's head, all of which is obvious enough, and very Baxterian.

The most important influences on Baxter's playwrighting, however, were the two French dramatists Sartre and Giraudoux and the classical Greek dramas. Baxter first became acquainted with Sartre's plays when he acted in Ngaio Marsh's production of *The Flies* in Christchurch in 1948. The experience remained with him, and he later described the production methods as "rigid" (the fixing of every single move by each actor), but "brilliant and mannered." *The Flies* and Giraudoux's *Tiger at the Gates* were his "springboard" in adapting from the original sources for his Greek plays (*Mr O'Dwyer's Dancing Party*, *The Sore-Footed Man*, *The Bureaucrat*, and *The Temptations of Oedipus*), because he had realized the dangers of attempting direct translation. McNaughton notes the effect of Giraudoux's *La Guerre de Troie n'aura pas lieu* on *The Sore-Footed Man* and of *Amphitryon 38* on the early scenes of Baxter's *The Runaway Wife*. Briefly, what Baxter thought he took into his late plays from these French sources is "a gloss and panache," an urbane surface, "a prose rhetoric with some precision and some use of poetic images." From Giraudoux in particular, a master of parallel and antithetical dialogue, he learned the technique of having characters together onstage, each expressing himself, as it were, in a different key, failing to communicate because each was narcissistically confined in his own world.

III Themes

When we turn to the substance of Baxter's plays, particularly his themes, we find ourselves on familiar, perhaps richer, ground. A list may make this clear: free will, death, religion, drunkenness, commitment, destitution, words, love, materialism, community, the lost garden, bureaucracy, marriage, existentialism. Perhaps the center of that ground is "the enigma of human freedom". "I began to realise many years ago," Baxter says in his introduction to *The Sore-Footed Man,* "that neither conventional ethics nor the theology of Aquinas were much use in determining what choices a man should make who wishes to win a war, or court a woman, or even free himself from the chains of family conditioning." Elsewhere he called "the question of the age . . . Whether man does or does not possess free will." Free will in a world of limited possibilities is the central theme of *The Wide Open Cage,* posited in Hogan, the drunken "Christ crucified," who is at once apparently helpless in a world mysteriously God-created and a victim of calculating contemporary society, where deliberate hypocrisy pays and the unwary are in bondage at once to their own appetites and to the chains created for them by fellow beings not haunted by conscience.

Odysseus in *The Sore-Footed Man* (whom Baxter feared, quite rightly, he had made a fascist) is the apparently conscienceless man of action and expediency. Philoctetes, whose wounded foot is the mark of his humanity, is a victim-figure, Odysseus' contrast. The risk-taking adventurer uses the security-seeking Philoctetes' own medium (talk) to persuade him that he can come to full life only by living in fear, taking risks, being insecure. This existential message leads Philoctetes (in any case bored with domesticity) into going back to Troy. Ambivalently, Odysseus' real aim had been to get hold of the bow of Hercules which Philoctetes now had, and incidentally Odysseus helps himself, as it were, to the "virtue" of Philoctetes' bored wife, Eunoe. How much freedom does Philoctetes' commitment show in him?

Polyneices and Eteocles, in *The Temptations of Oedipus,* are cruder pragmatists than Odysseus, the fascist general. Both these sons of Oedipus desire this world and jostle for its possession. Polyneices cannot understand his father's claim that dispossession of his kingdom has left him free. "Free?" says Polyneices, and Oedipus replies: "Free of hatred — free of money — free of plotting and swindling — free of the soldiers who are both guards and — free of the shirt of power that eats into the bones like acid." Oedipus' bursts of fretfulness at several points of the play might seem to deny this, but Baxter was never simplistic enough to believe that "freedom" is totally assertive and constant. In the same play, how free is Ismene? She has made her choice, just as her sister Antigone has chosen to share her father's destitution. Thus, the question of freedom is complex, and the condition is composed of both commitment and detachment. Perhaps for this reason *The Temptation of Oedipus* seems the most resonant of all Baxter's plays, for in it Oedipus is shown as, first, "condemned" to destitution, he has *fallen*. What the play comes down to, though, is an exploration of his discovery of the "freedom" inherent in suffering.

Many of Baxter's characters are drunks. He says of those in *The Band Rotunda* (p. viii): "It would be a mistake . . . to suppose that because the characters are drunks their inner states are radically different from those of their neighbours." McNaughton makes some interesting observations about such characters. He sees them as "pretty useless for conventional dramatic purposes . . . all vestiges of ambition knocked out of them. . . . They are cornered men, ready to scurry further behind their band rotunda the moment their dubious freedom is challenged" (188). This, however, is the nub of the whole matter, as McNaughton himself sees when he notes, "His colony of alcoholics is a microcosm." For the "conventional dramatic purposes" of expressionist drama the drunks seem a not inappropriate fit. "The only God I had came out of a bottle" says Skully from the depths of his "wide open cage," for the bottle assuages fear of the opening. Baxter's *ersatz* "Christ-figure" in *The Band Rotunda* is both a boozer and a homosexual, who robs the collection box for the sake of the lepers. Representative of Baxter's Graham Greene-like "theology," Snowy has in a vision encountered a white-robed figure who confronts him with two crosses, a black and a white, commanding him to choose: ". . . and I said, 'I don't mind which, Lord. It's your business, not mine.' And he said to me, 'Take up the black one, It's the cross of sin.' And so I picked it up and began to carry it. And the light went out" (46). Snowy has belief, not virtue, that is the point. Baxter's "black booze-rooster" presides over the sinful world.

Love and the various forms of lack-love, anti-love and vacuity are

Unveiling Chaos: Baxter's Drama

also central themes in Baxter's drama, though one of its thematic weaknesses is that the negative seems always much the more dominant. We glimpse a sense of human love in Skully's girlfriend Norah and in Oedipus' daughters, Ismene and Antigone, but just about everywhere else it is "grim demanding hags" and opportunists. More strongly and persistently portrayed is Hydra-headed anti-love, which is most obviously revealed in attitudes to marriage: the women's discussion of it in *Mr O'Dwyer's Dancing Party*, Ennis's dissatisfaction, and the Dionysian fantasies of O'Dwyer; the deadening effect of marriage, feared by both Norah and Skully in *The Wide Open Cage*; the marital division which is an aspect of both *The First Wife* and *Mr Brandywine Chooses a Gravestone*; the frustration in marriage sketched out in *The Devil and Mr Mulcahy;* and the mutual dissatisfaction of Philoctetes and Eunoe in *The Sore-Footed Man* (perhaps, after all, Philoctetes took his snake-bitten foot back to Troy merely to get away).

Another manifestation of the anti-love theme is in the linked treatments of expediency and bureaucracy. "It's the churches that put man in a cage," cries Skully, thinking of the institution. Later he says, "the unconscious hypocrite is the world's worst killer" (for his puritan moralism leads to nullity), but in two late plays, *The Sore-Footed Man* and *The Temptations of Oedipus*, Baxter portrays conscious hypocrites in Odysseus and Theseus (so much for each as a putative hero). Each dissembles in the service of an institution, each uses other people, and in each (or the idea of each) one encounters a tangible lack of the sense of other human beings. To Odysseus it is expedient to obtain the bow, so with the help of the biddable Neoptolemus, he will turn any trick to do it. The Theseus in Baxter's free adaptation of *Oedipus at Colonnus* is seen by his Athenians as balanced, practical, inventive, and a believer in correct procedure and appropriate ceremony. In contrast to Oedipus, who holds that, "To be punished is to be confirmed in existence," Theseus dissimulates to a mob, at the same time ruling it iron-fistedly. The play's focus is Oedipus' state of mind, his view of human affairs. Unlike the Athenian citizens, who worship the grove of the Gentle Ones from afar, Oedipus is willing to commit himself fully to life. Finally, not without querulousness, he learns to value the state of destitution, for to be in it is "to know what man is." Man's condition is calamitous bcause it involves human love and "to love is to hope and to hope is to fear." Hope for love and desire for inertia continually struggle in Baxter's Oedipus. Not surprisingly, when

Athens is threatened by plague its citizens see Oedipus' presence as the probable cause. Expedient as always, Theseus the manager hits on the idea of making a propitiatory sacrifice of Antigone's child. Oedipus in protest cries out, "Can't you see the child is the future?" Failing to prevent Theseus, observer of forms, speaker of the proper words, appeaser of the mob he despises, from proceeding with his inhuman plan, Oedipus in a flash of thunder gives himself up to Poseidon. What, in the end, has he learned of life? Antigone feels that he would be pleased the plague had ceased to bother the Athenians, that he had learned perhaps of kindliness and mercy, but Ismene shares in a deeper knowledge. She says, "Father would not have been...," and the lights fade with Theseus and Antigone looking at her in puzzlement and surprise.

Human bafflement and inconsistency are integral to *The Temptations of Oedipus*, as also is a critique of materialism. Oedipus is torn between kingship and brotherhood; Ismene confuses *eros* and *agape*. Part of the dire message is that the seekers after wholeness dwell in confusion, whereas the hunters for material power are clear-headed. "Hang him at the town gate!" is Theseus' immediate response to the protester, and when Oedipus advises his son to abandon the quest for kingship and become a husbandman, Polyneices replies, "I see no vineyard in this place; only an old man in rotting clothes..." (74).

Naturally, religion is a major theme in Baxter's plays. "We're each of us in a cage till Judgment Day," says Father Tom O'Shea to Jack Skully early in *The Wide Open Cage*. But Skully, who describes a skull as "the only certain friend I've got" and declares that the only God he knows came out of a bottle, is not so easily satisfied. "Why did you make us?" He asks, "Make us with a mind as big as the sky and a dirty hole to live in?" (15). Skully's counterpart in *The Band Rotunda* is Concrete Grady. In both plays the central figure is tough, sensing the *possibility* of God perhaps, but skeptical, questioning. Next to them, in each case, is a "Christ-figure" (Hogan in *The Wide Open Cage*, Lindsay in *The Band Rotunda*) — a being with a strong sense of God, the god-in-man, but mired in human flaws (hence the repeated linking of Baxter with Graham Greene, both exploring a "theology" in which the confirmed sinner is the bearer of grace). Skully's "Why did you make us?" corresponds to Con Grady's musing: "Maybe we'll be drinking plonk in Heaven one day. But I don't *know* — if you want a name for it, Jock, I'm a Catholic agnostic." Toward the end of the play he says, "The World's all right. It's us that have got twisted" (59); twisted into alienation, so: "It's no paradise together — but it's worse the other way." "Things go out of joint because we don't think straight," he adds, and, "God's not the only god. Man's / god, too. If we started thinking straight, we could do just about anything. We could help each other" (59), though each is responsible for himself. Jock declares his belief in "the brotherhood of man," Rosie her feeling that "one decent man" could put the world right, but the last word belongs to Concrete Grady. Rosie says to him, "You think too much. You think you're God, Grady. You bring him back to life then. Bring him back to life" (64), and the play closes, with fine ambiguity, on Grady's words: "Jock dead. Poor Jock. He was alive a minute ago. (*Loudly*). Where have you gone to? Can't you see we're all dying? We can't do a bloody thing. We haven't got the strength for it or the brains. . . . Come down from your bloody cross. . . . Come down, you dirty mad old bugger! Come down and be buried." Conscious of the potentially offensive nature of this, Baxter once said in a talk, "That ejaculation can no doubt be theologically justified in terms of the terrible and mysterious saying of Saint Paul, that Christ was made sin for us."

Snowy had been referred to earlier as a "dirty mad old bugger." He is God, Jock is God, Concrete Grady himself is God — the God who to save man must be crucified yet again. As the scene fades, Grady sprawls on the concrete steps of the Band Rotunda, his Golgotha, exhausted momentarily in the climb to his own Passion.

"There's no god inside Philoctetes," Eunoe disparages in *The Sore-Footed Man*. Otherwise, the gods seem to have little part in that play of human expediencies, but Skully and Grady are different; one can feel the God, if not inside them, hovering nearby. Having rejected sociological and "realistic" forms of drama, Baxter eventually cleaved to another myth-form, the Christian liturgy. In a beautiful image in his introduction he describes *The Band Rotunda* (a location reminiscent of altar and tabernacle) as formally choral and episodic. Of the actors' movement onstage he says: "I compared this movement to the whirling of leaves on a winter pavement, or the eddying movement of the souls blown across the dark sky of the First Circle of Dante's nferno" (p. viii). His characters are "methos" (drunks addicted to methylated spirits), but they share the illusions of humans generally. "Their central problem is, as for us, the incommunicable weight of life itself."

In *The Devil and Mr Mulcahy* Baxter again explores his theme, that the human agents of God are not coldly perfectionist but fallible and sinful, and he sees the "hero" Mulcahy as somewhat diffidently presenting "a humanist Catholicism which allows for human disorder and growth" (p. ix), to which contrasts the death-dealing fundamentalism of Paul Marshall and "The Seed of Light" and the self-interested efforts of Simon and Rachel to construct a nature-religion around Golden Eye the hawk. Mrs. Marshall, one of the characters who crop up in the plays who voice nostalgia for the childhood garden, has a view of human nature somewhat akin to Grady's. God's "flawed mirror," for wholeness it needs the *aroha*, or tribal love, which Mulcahy so disastrously tries to promote.

All the ideas are Baxter's, traceable throughout his work. God or gods are working within us, though we so often fail to recognize their presence; but in our split universe (or perception of it) Calvinism or Jansenism appear to be impossible to quell; they merely take other forms "like a body swelling with another kind of life as it decomposes" (p. ix). No wonder, then, that the communal foundation of drama is human limitation rather than Divine light. Yet the focus of drama, for Baxter, always comes back to the nature of selfhood, which is why he considers all drama "religious," for he felt that all self-projections were manifestations of the gods within, a showing forth from "the incurable pantheism of the human soul," and at the same time from the abyss or the void. Snowy Lindsay says, "Concrete Grady, the world's got no centre." It is at the hollow center that the individual must discover himself. Baxter's attempts to project that center onto a theater stage are notable, at their best, for a somber poetry, a probing vigor, and genuine compassion.

CHAPTER 9

The Way to the Upper Room

WITH youthful detachment, Baxter was able to write in *Blow, Wind of Fruitfulness:*

> I often think
> Of the climb we made like beetles up a drain
> From neanderthal, to be washed down again
> In a flood of dirty water from the sink.
> Lions and horses also sport a brain
> But do not pine for a celestial stink.
>
> (44)

The path from a lost Eden seemed to lead to an "obliterating sea" or a choice between "an antique cosmology" and "hostile night" (PU, 18). Yet already then he accepted the world as "His flawed mirror," and read Ursula Bethell as a Christian for whom "the natural world was the mirror and self-revelation of the Holy Spirit" (*Trends*, 13). From this time on he had a double view of nature. As he put it in "Literature and Belief": "The whole visible creation, which we are bound to believe is the work of His Hands . . . shows magnificent, delicate and exquisite art in every detail" (MH, 42). Alongside this he continued in a fatalistic view of human experience: the world we are presented with (or, at least, perceive) is Chaos manifest, once we have left "the green inn." Amid that chaos Jesus and Mary are consolation.

I *The Veil of Consciousness*

Perhaps his life shaped itself so that the two views are reconciled? Discussing Allen Curnow's verse-drama *The Axe* in *Trends*, he suggests that "for Curnow as for D. H. Lawrence the original sin is consciousness," the particular fate of Adam and Eve. Baxter's view is similar, but at first he refused on behalf of artists any link with an institutionalized attempt to overcome the Fallen condition. Of the "pure artist" he says: "His social aim . . . is that every City should become a Wilderness. The aim of the doctrinaire artist, Christian or Communist, is that every Wilderness should be contained in the Just City. My sympathy is with the former, as I consider conformity a great deal more dangerous than non-conformity" (*Trends*, 17).

Chapman, Weir, and others see a positive Christian element in *The Fallen House*, but Chapman feels that, "Mr Baxter seems to admire and covet belief rather than to have it" (*Landfall* [1953], 212), asking: "Has Calvin, in Mr Baxter's view, interposed between affection and desire leaving them broken apart, thus making expulsion from the green Eden not time's work but the serpent's?", Chapman answers his own question: "He suggests them all and wisely settles for none." *The Fallen House* also carries intimations of a veil between human experience and the actual state of earthly perfection:

> O out of this rock tomb
> Of labyrinthine grief, I start and cry
> Toward his real day: The undestroyed
> Fantastic Eden of a waking dream
> (FH, 19)

"Real day" becomes "green cradle" in "Poem By the Clock Tower, Sumner," where "Again the dark dove nestles in my breast" (FH, 21). In a sonnet "To My Wife" Baxter promotes their "married fondness" as his most cherished human experience, yet draws again on the image of the flawed mirror to set it in a universal context as "a looking-glass/ That dully shows the uncreated Light," which will be fully created "In His eternal day" (FH, 37). God's love, in "Lazarus" (FH, 32) is characterized forebodingly as something beyond human love and "more to be feared than wrath." Yet other poems in the book, such as "Thrushes" and "Revenants" (which speaks of "oblivion's gristmill") carry forward a note of determinism.

By then clearly the life-giving river and Eden garden had continuing significance for Baxter. This side of the veil New Zealand has its particular place, to cite his editorial for *Numbers* (November 1954), "Dante in the Antipodes." One (presumably Baxter himself) says:

The Way to the Upper Room 151

"I'd say he wrote about spiritual states, states of being. You've missed out Limbo and Purgatory anyway. All the dry, canny intellectuals went to Limbo. They sat on a green lawn and discussed Philosophy. Inside hell gate. But in order to get to Purgatory he went round and round the Pit, right to the bottom, and came out by a little rock stair in the antipodes. Maybe New Zealand." (2)

The writer's Purgatory in New Zealand is the struggle to maintain creative freedom in the face of Mrs. Grundyism, source of many struggles between the institutional church and the artist. In *The Fire and the Anvil* Baxter traces the need for such struggle back to a Manichean element in Christianity, which he sums up as "the old dream that man's freedom is to be found by release from his body, rather than by acts of prayer and labour in a material world" (FA, 46). As to the artist's purpose: "Modern man desires as much to be delivered from an uncreative society as from his sins" (FA, 48), and in that regard the enemy is "that great incubus of the marshes, the master State."

II Developing Christianity

A few years later (just before his conversion to Catholicism) Baxter spoke (in "To God the Son" [IFN, 47]) of his "false forced praise," and asked: "Teach that obedience which I lack the most, Obedience to love." He spent a period in the Trappist monastery at Kopua, Hawke's Bay, where a monk told him: "Jimmy, they say that when we come here first, God gives us bread and butter and honey; then, after a while, he takes away the honey; then, the butter; and sometimes, the bread as well" (MH, 11), and this could well sum up the stages of Baxter's spiritual journey thenceforth.

Christian feeling permeates the texture of the new poems in *Howrah Bridge and Other Poems*, together with the view of human experience implied in the title of "Ballad of Calvary Street." What is endured in Calvary Street now begins to acquire possible positive value, that of personal destitution, of humans enduring the *"fire/ Where affliction makes them whole"* (HB, 27). Recollection of youthful pleasure, or looking to the future by "talk with angels," these are "stony rapture," without sustenance. Passive resignation is more dangerous than the self-flagellation of a St. Simeon Stylites. The maxim Baxter puts in the peddler's mouth in "The Tempters," *"Thirst, obey, endure,"* speaks for more than mere passivity.

Again we arrive at the crucial *Pig Island Letters*, the whole framework of which is religious, beginning from a sense of human circumscription. The human universe is "God's body blazing on damnation's tree," and the Christian life is seen in each case as taking form from Christ's Passion. Absence of "coherent love," consciousness of death, these are the prime evidences of human suffering, inevitable because of man's perception of his world "through the dark prism of self-love" (PIL, 15). Even this egomania may be overcome by faith.

Again we witness a view of the human faculties as limiting and distorting. For Baxter, Mary became a chief means of recovering "the single vision." Devoted to her, he yet prays in "The Rock Woman" to the woman "unvirgin," "all-suffering," who is "pain's torso," the sinful aspect of the Mother. *The Rock Woman* closes with a statement of resignation, faith:

> Yet hard for human blood
> Is the habit of relinquishment,
> Abandoning of Isaac to the knife
> That tortured Abraham. Come now;
> Poems are trash, the flesh I love will die,
> Desire is bafflement,
> But one may say that Father Noah kept
> Watch while the wild beasts slept,
>
> Not knowing even if the land would rise
> Out of the barren waves.
> That ark I keep, that watch on the edge of sleep
> While the dark water heaves.
>
> (RW, 86)

III The Flowering Cross

Published in the same year as *The Rock Woman*, *The Flowering Cross* is in no way a literary work, but stems from the catechetical activity which Baxter undertook near the end of his career as a playwright (1968). Two central views are sustained in it, but one of these at least with a different emphasis.

Prepared to admit that sensory knowledge may be illusory, he realizes that so are "the Utopian promises of scientists and politicians, and my own power of reason" (FC, 8), and so is our supposed knowledge of other human souls. But faith in God is "neutral to reason," evinced by the will, yet finally a gift from God Himself.

Perhaps the greatest value of *The Flowering Cross* is its detailed

The Way to the Upper Room

documentation of Baxter's view of the church at a late stage in his life. A proselytizer on its behalf, he sees the church both as his authority and as a rather clumsy instrument of the faith, potentially antagonistic to artistic freedom (a subject he had dealt with on several earlier occasions, to the same end) and in opposition to some, at least, of the life-giving attributes of natural man.

A whole range of church doctrine and attitude is dealt with. Late in the book are brief pieces on Purgatory, Hell, and Heaven. Purgatory, he says, is a state of relief, for the sufferer therein is assured of Heaven. Hell, manifest even in Paradise as the fountain of the tears of the damned, was an intolerable doctrine to him. Taking the traditional position, he professes belief in it but is curiously evasive. He hopes Hell's fiery lake is populated only by demons. Having denied that Purgatory is experienced in this life, he now says that Hell is. His view of Heaven is a kind of reversal of this, for he sees it as a place where all our cherished earthly activities continue, but in a state of perfection, which would be ours already were it not for the Fall.

Human beings today are under a second curse, as Baxter wrote to John Weir in 1962, the falsifying and sterilizing pretense that there never was a Fall. His admiration for natural man is due, in part, to the feeling that he "remembers, as if in a dream, his first state" (MH, 20), but modern man has lost such a vision, preferring a laundered view. But to be humanly conscious is to be maimed, incoherent, incomplete. Salvation is the overcoming of these defects. Primarily, this is achieved through love, but love itself has an important other face, that of resignation. Once we acknowledge the Fall as event, we must accept it as our Cross.

Closely related to man's Fallen state is his mortal nature. The stark question is put in *The Flowering Cross:* "in the face of obvious physical death, what reason have we to believe in heaven?" (FC, 154). For the young Baxter, death was "utter and final" (BP, 15). When, a few years later, he declares, "I am man, child no longer/ And I accept my death" (BWF, 14), this (as its mechanical rhythm perhaps betrays) is rhetoric. Other early poems, such as "Tarras Moon" and "The Morgue" speak fear of death, and even the beautiful cadences of "The Fallen House" portray an obliterative, fear-ridden death. Yet in *Pig Island Letters* acceptance of mortality is a key element, for example, in "Waipatiki Beach," of which Weir says: "What Baxter found in the natural scene of Waipatiki Beach was an unmistakable sign of the presence of death, that event which brings a final order to the chaos of living" (31). The note is sounded in the book's title poem and again in "At Rotorua" (PIL, 28) and "East Coast Journey" (PIL, 24):

> As a man
> Grows older he does not want beer, bread, or the prancing flesh,
> But the arms of the eater of life, Hine-nui-te-po.

IV The Last Phase Begins

"The first Mass that was ever celebrated," Baxter wrote in 1969, "was celebrated by Christ Himself in the Upper Room the day before His death on the cross. And as a result of His action, something existed which had never existed before — namely, the Blessed Sacrament . . ." (FC, 175). In the name of that Sacrament, Baxter was to become a barefoot, long-coated, long-bearded figure, somewhat resembling the Tolstoy of the last days, vowed to poverty and to becoming "father" of his family of *nga mokai* by the Wanganui River. Activist Christianity began to consume his whole being.

After the Dunedin years he set off very much like Christian in the opening pages of *The Pilgrim's Progress*, who cried out, "Life! Life! Eternal Life!" Six months of solitary meditation in the old-established Catholic mission settlement of Jerusalem (Hiruharama) preceded his founding there of the commune for drop-outs and troubled youths. His respect for, and interest in, the Maoris deepened. He became Hemi, new-named, as if to signify new-born. During his last few years he produced an impressive group of published writings and, although they are demonstrably ancillary to his main concerns, our chief object is to assess them and their place in the canon. Apart from publication of the plays and *The Tree House*, a book of poems for children, there is a small collection of published radio talks, *The Six Faces of Love*, and seven separate poetry titles.

To set a context we may use, as Tony Simpson does in a perceptive article,[1] Baxter's own rationale for his communal activities, given in one of these talks:

> I have been engaged for some time, with the help of God, in an experiment that involves the Love of the Many. In the haphazard community that has grown up where I live, there are one or two principles that seem necessary and permanent. . . .
> If we are to rebuild the sacramental universe our civilisation has shattered

to pieces — I see no way of doing it except by sharing the things we possess. Then we are using them as God wishes them to be used. . . .
Another principle, is that people should love one another, and display love in a physical manner. There are good reasons behind this.[2]

Though truncated, this gives a factual sense of the late-period Baxter, Hemi the millenarian. It should be stressed, and will become evident, that Baxter lived deeply, and died, for these precepts.

V   Jerusalem Sonnets

In *Jerusalem Sonnets* (1970) he established the serviceable two-line unrhyming stanza which became the chief medium of his Jerusalem poems, the line itself at core a pentameter shaken loose of formal restriction. (He had begun to use the form as early as the mid-sixties.) The work's strength is certainly not in "making it new," and Baxter here further confines (and defines) his scope by adhering to the fourteen-line sonnet length, even though otherwise ignoring the traditional form. If he is not "masturbating his ego" (in a phrase of Simpson's) he is very much at the center of the sequence, what he does and what he suffers. But there is a new kind of integrity. Rhetoric has been burned off, and the simplistic has become simplicity. As Murray Edmond justly says, "by the time of the *Jerusalem Sonnets* Baxter didn't give a damn about his style as he had in the past. The mask of style — the accepted notion of what poetry is — has been dropped to reveal the man himself, guileless."[3] The familiar claim for many a bad current versifier is hereby put before us. A long acquaintanceship with Baxter, and some measure of friendship, makes me hesitate over "guileless." Either for the form or the content (to engage momentarily that so often fruitless dichotomy) one could see him as most guileful, but he has a style so natural and immediate to himself and his concerns that it seems, as literary or artistic sheen, to have evaporated.

No peak moments of high rhetoric grace these thirty-nine sonnets. What matters is what Baxter is thinking about and, equally, how: his devotion to the Lord (a Christian Lord, but Maori in His names: *Te Atua* — God, *Te Ariki* — Christ, The Lord, *Te Matua* — The Father, *Te Tama* — The Son). The self-mythologizing Baxter reaches his consummation in the obvious and unfolding circumstance that he receives his own experience in a consciousness at least partly Maori. He lives like a Desert Father, in poverty, doing back-breaking fieldwork, lice in his beard, crabs in his crotch, scourging his body, discovering that "to be is to die/ The death of others." Private reference — to Jill, Maori Johnny, Allan Thornton, Boyle Crescent, and so on avoids the irritating flavor of evoking an "in-group" milieu. We are long familiar with the kind of people who are Baxter's concern. Boyle Crescent (location of the Auckland doss-house) is "The junkies' pigeon-roost, / House of sorrow, house of love." Among such he places his own struggle and self-indulgence:

> To give away cigarettes,
> That's the hard one, Colin!
>
> To live on rolled oats, raisins,
> Potatoes, milk, raw cabbage,
>
> It's even a pleasure — but I confess I need a smoke
> More than I need a woman!
>
> It's more like breathing — ever since I broached the guests' tobacco
> (Along with the guests) I've been a doomed man!
>
> Perhaps earlier yet — at six years old,
> When I kept what I stole from my father in a rusty tin
>
> Under the house, mixed with old rotted
> Cabbage tree fibres — was it original virtue
>
> Or original sin? I roll it now, and draw deep
> The herb of darkness, preferring Nirvana to Heaven.
>
> (JS, s. 15)

The sequence has unobtrusive shape, beginning with the protagonist's sense of his own suffering, and his advice from the Curé d'Ars, that love is the way to "hack down the wall of God". His concerns are poverty of self, seeking comfort in God, its elusiveness in this life, but the rare moment always possible of love shared, "With our weapons thrown down, for a breathing space" (s. 13). In midsequence there is an animadversion against newspapers (s. 16), spreaders of the modern sickness, but this is soon followed by a tender affirmation of the desire to do God's will (s. 18). Sonnet 20 works beautifully around the tradition of Christ the Fish, through a figure of three fish on a finger ring:

> ... say the single one is the pakeha fish
>
> And the big one Te Ariki
> Followed by te tuna, the Maori fish

The Way to the Upper Room

> Who twists on after Him in poverty and darkness,
> And I must go with them upstream to the heart of the cross.

Other sonnets are a prayer for an older brother (*tuakana*), for freedom from pride; on the twin rivers of love and materialism, the "*taniwha* in the heart" and the river which provides "Rides for tourists on the jetboat at Pipiriki," and this contrast appears again, with sensitivity, in the latter part of Sonnet 27:

> there was a girl
>
> Who sat beside me there;
> She would hold a blue flower at the centre of the bullring
>
> While the twigs on the tree became black
> And then slowly green again — she was young — if I had said
>
> "Have my coat; have my money" —
> She would have gone away; but because I gave her nothing
>
> She came again and again to share that nothing
> Like a bird that nests in the open hand.

The personal force in such writing may happily be described as "guileless"; it also betokens a profound confidence in what one is, and what one is doing.

Only at sonnet 28 does Baxter refer directly to the founding of a tribe. Continuing without break from the instance of shared destitution quoted above, he plunges the reader into "a room full of smoke," and considers the nature, purpose, and effectiveness of such a place and his relation to it (suggesting as epitaph his newfound Maori name, " 'Hemi' —/ And nothing else" (s. 29). As the sequence draws to an end he identifies more closely with Christ, offering sacrifice of himself (s. 34) toward founding love's tribe:

> They say it is best
>
> To break a rotten egg in the creek
> To get eels — I think I am that egg
>
> And Te Ariki must crack me open
> If the fish are to be drawn in at all.
> (s. 35)

The four sonnets which close the sequence rise to a remarkable pitch of eloquence, at once controlled and free. Sonnets 36 and 37 speak of the protagonist's total self-surrender to God, adjuring himself:

> Be glad you can distinguish not an inch of the track,
>
> That the stones are sharp, that your hide can itch,
> That His true weight is heavy on your back.

"The bright coat of art he has taken away from me," he says; "Rule over myself he has taken away from me" (s. 37). Yet, as C. K. Stead so justly remarks,[4] these poems have a subtle beauty, of accurately observed details suffused with genuine feeling and humor, the sonnets being interdependent and therefore to be received as a whole. Identifying with one of the thieves who died with Christ on the cross (s. 38), the protagonist says, "There is not even judgment any more/ In the place where I have to be," and the sequence closes offered as a gift "From Hiruharama,/ From Hemi te tutua" (From Jerusalem, from James the nobody). But an immensity of judgment, a lifetime's, is in the texture of these poems. Here Baxter's notable rhetoric is completely in service to the conviction of his whole experience; yet he is no propagandist, no proselytizer. Clearly, graced with moments of high simple beauty, the sequence gives an account of his spiritual struggles and his vision of a tribe. For all the suffering which permeates the work, we witness in it the overt beginnings of a profound metamorphosis.

VI Jerusalem Daybook

In *Jerusalem Daybook* (1971) Baxter again used his newfound "sonnet" form but in conjunction with other verse-forms and heavily interspersed with prose. "In this daybook," he says, "I offer only a bundle of anecdotes, intuitions and conjectures — points where the shell of my own egocentricity has been broken through by the occasions of communal life. These points may be felt as wounds. But wounds are necessary" (p. 2). What absorbs him is "a theology of communality," one in which proper detachment is maintained (from one's own ego), while through experiment, mistakes, successes, eventually is discovered "the communal Christ."

Throughout Baxter's association with it, the Jerusalem commune was subject of many newspaper articles and reports, a surprising number being genuine attempts to come to terms with the "experiment"; but the community was beset from two sides, the

The Way to the Upper Room

"national paranoia" (essentially, secular puritanism) and the local community, particularly "The Holy Neighbours" (p. 25). These are an essential part of the context of *Jerusalem Daybook*.

The whole book is pervaded by the spirit of humility, poverty (destitution), and acceptance. If we are to remain within our customary categories, it is perhaps more a religious work than a work of literature. Interspersed with poems, the prose has no rhetorical pretensions and no particular distinction, unless directness and clarity be so regarded. The matter of it derives from Baxter's lifelong concerns, here dealt with in a spirit of culmination.

For the young he fears "impalement on the stake of an undesired education," a theme he returns to from a variety of angles. When the Maori elder Potini tells him, "I had very little education," Hemi replies, "Thank God for that." Of one of *nga mokai* ("the fatherless"), he says: "Her Daddy has promised her a new car when she gets her degree. There is plenty of money and social prestige in her home. It is her job to add the kudos of education" (p. 35). Such families he finds "the strongest juggernaut of our times." He pities the children, "who try to love one another, and even us as well, in the terrible social graveyard we have helped to construct for them" (p. 37). Baxter, apparently, saw himself as trying to found a tribe free of the bureaucracy, free of the fetters of social custom and bourgeois ambition.

Three-quarters prose, loosely meditative, *Jerusalem Daybook*'s central theme (which had been touched upon in *The Temptations of Oedipus* and elsewhere) is poverty, which is also freedom. Speaking of the "desacralised, depersonalised, centralised Goliath" of contemporary, anticommunal society, Baxter says:

> I do not relish the role of David, in confronting that Goliath, who numbs the soul wherever he touches it. But I find myself curiously, perhaps absurdly, cast in that role. And the five water-worn stones I choose from the river, to put in my sling, are five spiritual aspects of Maori communal life —
> arohanui: the Love of the Many;
> manuhiritanga: hospitality to the guest and stranger;
> korero: speech that begets peace and understanding;
> matewa: the night life of the soul;
> mahi: work undertaken from communal love.
> I do not know what the outcome of the battle will be. My aim may be poor. But I think my weapons are well chosen.
>
> (JD, 54)

The book has no literary pretensions and structurally resembles a string of beads. Opening with a statement of his own dual nature, as revealed in two dreams — himself as solitary, himself as "engineer" (of a ship), he goes on to consider the vital difference between commune ("the works of Caesar are sub-personal") and community (a seed planted by Te Wairua Tapu — the Holy Spirit). One aspect of community is a painful confrontation of oneself, which can lead (contrary to idealistic picturings of harmony and love) to misanthropy, but beyond that to the deep love it is worth dying for.

He turns next to New Zealand society and remarks on its involvement in mass killings (Vietnam) and yet the strange vacuity of that involvement: "We Antipodeans are an innocent people. Yet I think our peculiar absence of guilt may be a heavier burden to carry than the guilt itself" (p. 8). What is denied such a society is the privilege of religious suffering. What it suffers instead is a life-negating puritanism, but: "Meanwhile the wicked world goes on healing the wicked world." From a brotherhood of poverty derives *agape* (the Maori *aroha*) and the freedom from anxiety of those in God's hands. For responsibility he substitutes "availability," being accessible to God's will: "If he wants the community to survive, then it will survive; if not then it won't.... He doesn't require my anxiety. And I have noticed that anxiety impairs one's judgment" (p. 12 - 13).

What God "requires" is one's love of one's fellows, dying to oneself (everywhere in these late works Baxter's actual death is very present to him). Double conversion had left him with a sense of himself as a "nobody," his soul a leper, his body (likened to an old *kumara*, Maori potato) the instrument for demonstrating the unimportance, limitations, and sufferings of dwelling in the human universe. "I am a coarse man by intention," he says, and relates an anecdote about farting, which he calls "shooting angels" (reminiscent of Joyce's *Portrait of the Artist* and, for that matter, Osborne's *Luther*). Why does he "shoot angels"? " 'The Church Fathers used to say that the Fall of Angels left room for the human race to go to Heaven. So...' " (p. 27), and the anecdote against angelism serves to illustrate his anti-elitism and anti-institutionalism. Against mankind-stifling rules, he nonetheless firmly believed in "the Law," that is, the Christian code above and beyond mere Church doctrine and institution: "Love is crucified on the Law till the end of time. The Law is necessary; without the Law there would be no Cross" (p. 29).

Such is the tenor of *Jerusalem Daybook*, which touches also upon

The Way to the Upper Room 161

the "theology of kenosis" (self-emptying, to make room for God), the similarity between LSD ("It restores a sacred universe," p. 37) and the practice of poverty, poverty and passive resistance, poverty and property (theft, possessiveness, treating another person as "property"), poverty and the human parasite ("No person is replaceable./ The bludgers and parasites are god's gift to us . . ."; p. 43).

Jerusalem is set in a bend of the Wanganui River. The book ends with a poem "In Praise of the Taniwha" (the river spirit, invoked in relation to love in *Jerusalem Sonnets*). Swimming naked (a natural right, but a social problem) he is conscious of the *taniwha* ("water spirit"), seeks its protection, regarding it as "a principle in nature and in the human soul" (p. 52). He had retained the life-giving animism referred to twenty years earlier in *Recent Trends in New Zealand Poetry*.

I have not singled out the book's poems for particular comment and will say only that they merge into the general easy and unpretentious style (assimilated from "street language") and are integral:

> Hard, heavy, slow, dark,
> Or so I find them, the hands of Te Whaea
>
> Teaching me to die. Some lightness will come later
> When the heart has lost its unjust hope
>
> For special treatment. Today I go with a bucket
> Over the paddocks of young grass,
>
> So delicate like fronds of maidenhair,
> Looking for mushrooms, I find twelve of them,
>
> Most of them little, and some eaten by maggots,
> But they'll do to add to the soup. It's a long time now
>
> Since the great ikons fell down,
> God, Mary, home, sex, poetry,
>
> Whatever one uses as a bridge
> To cross the river that has only one beach,
>
> And even one's name is a way of saying —
> "This gap inside a coat" — the darkness I call God,

> The darkness I call Te Whaea, how can they translate
> The blue calm evening sky that a plane tunnels through
>
> Like a little wasp, or the bucket in my hand,
> Into something else? I go on looking
>
> For mushrooms in the field, and the fist of longing
> Punches my heart, until it is too dark to see.
>
> (JD, 23 - 24)

VII   Letter to Peter Olds

Letter to Peter Olds (1972) is based on the same "sonnet" form, but is antithetical to *Jerusalem Daybook*, which closes with the prayer, "bring us to Te Whaea, to the Mother of all men, to the void and the Beginning." This *Letter* opens by evoking "our terrible Mother, that stone Medusa / Sitting on her hill of skulls," and it considers again the problem of being a loving individual amid "the social circus." By no means a major work, this brief sequence has what Baxter once termed "incandescence," and a typical mixture of luridness, gentleness, literary knowingness, and easy colloquialism. Preaching the message of brotherly love, it is both characteristically gratuitous ("Have a wank for me," etc.) and pervasively and felicitously tender:

> When I climb the ladder to the upper bunk
> Perhaps I am a tribal shaman
>
> Climbing the tentpole to the country of the sky
> So that the dead can use his voice, —
>
> Does he find a woman there? Well, that could happen,
> But mainly, I think, it is the love of friends
>
> Plants the tentpole, builds the walls of the house,
> And will outlast with luck the fires of Armageddon.
>
> (s. 7)

In a late letter to his mother, he remarked that Kendrick Smithyman had said Baxter's best poems were those addressed to a single individual, and this may account for the number of poem-epistles he wrote in this period. Several appear in the posthumously published *The Labyrinth* (1974), and Max Harris, the Australian editor of *Angry Penguins*, combined two (to Sam Hunt and himself) into *Two Obscene Poems* (1973?). Each in rhymed couplets, neither adds anything of note to the canon, though it is worth noting that Harris judged Baxter to be "the finest poet of our time in our immediate horizon...." But because he is a New Zealander he is "not as well-known as he might be."[5]

VIII Autumn Testament

Two-thirds of *Autumn Testament* (1972) is taken up with the title poem, which otherwise resembles *Jerusalem Daybook* in being a mixture of prose and poetry. The simple opening sequence, "He Waiata Mo Te Kare" (A Song for Te Kare) is addressed to his wife: "You in Wellington,/ I at Jerusalem, / / Woman, it is my wish, / Our bodies should be buried in the same grave." It deals also with the historical and institutionalized church, seen as *pakeha*, contrasting it with the "church" as known at Hiruharama, the act of being there: "Wahi Ngaro: the void out of which all things come. That is where I find my peace.... it might seem that one has become an atheist.... Yet.... We do not create God by thinking about him" ("Notes", p. 5).

Day-to-day living at Hiruharama contrasts with the desacralization, depersonalization, and centralization (already mentioned elsewhere), which are "the three chief scourges of the urban culture." A parallel contrast involves personal relationships:

> Those we knew when we were both young,
> None of them have stayed together,
> All their marriages battered down....
>
> I was a gloomy drunk.
> You were a troubled woman . . .
> Yet our love did not turn to hate....
>
> I never wanted another wife.

The personal facts of Baxter's life are not our immediate concern, except that they are more and more explicitly the stuff of his writing in the last years. Not merely a complex personality but a divided one, for most of his adult days he was a walking war between an acute sense of the sacramental and a bundle of appetites. Frequently, once he had begun to grapple with his alcoholism in the later 1950s, he referred to it in his writings and possibly still occasionally succumbed to it. Reference to his sexual life is less explicit, perhaps more reticent, though the early relationship with "Pyrrha," mentioned in the poems, is followed by more or less vague references to relationships with other women (quite frequently more companionate than sexual). Obviously enough, Baxter had sexual affairs (their range and nature is not relevant here), and, on the road at last to Jerusalem, he eventually gave up living regularly with his family. Yet the exceptional fact remains that love and respect, on both sides, seemed to persist in his marriage until the end of his life. (These observations are made in response to the deeply personal nature of Baxter's late work.) When he was in Wellington he usually stayed in the family house and many times expressed the wish to have "Te Kare" at Hiruharama. His desire for this became part of the fabric of his life there. One of his reasons for leaving Wellington was pilgrimage, but the other was deep distrust of middle-class marriage and the resulting existence: "Be married and go mad; or be single and stay sane. The choice is Draconian. The problem is not lack of love. . . . The problem is lack of community" (AT, 7).

"Autumn Testament" (the title poem) is a rambling poetic and meditative journal, without particularly striking coherence as a piece of writing, but rather held together by the spirit of the man who wrote it. A recurring concern, especially in the early sections, is with the need for food, a perhaps not unconscious parallel with the need for spiritual sustenance. The poem begins from the reopening of the Jerusalem *wharepuni* (meetinghouse), which Hemi sees as a way-station on the journey to accepting *Wahi Ngaro* (the Void). Yet this way-station is a true community, and the great misfortune is loneliness: "The darkness of oneself returns/ Now that the house is empty." Being with others, the giving away of oneself to the point of total poverty and in genuine love — this is what assuages, though it can never totally appease, the "old hunger." Only death, return to the sea-god Tangaroa, or the graveyard (or a woman's breast, death of the self) can do that. Musing on death reminds him of his dead father in "the kingdom of summer stars," and of his own foolish longing for Heaven ("The wish to climb a ladder to the loft / Of God dies hard in us"). Insidious hunger is itself attachment to the things of this world, such as the pinewood grove he used to pray in during his first six months at Jerusalem, which is now being cleared for use as timber (s. 13). Turning again to his father's spirit, he asks: "is it easier to fight / The military machine, or the maggot of one's own heart?"

The Way to the Upper Room   165

Hunger is at the poem's core, however. Hunger for community (even, most hopefully, "the Church becoming human, / As if religion were not the cemetery of hope"; (s. 15); but the church is a bureaucratic institution. Like the Public Works Department and the Labour Bureau, it is one of the "lion's dens." In sonnets 17 and 18 he meditates on this hunger in its materialist transformation, in which one grasps for oneself rather than learning to "nourish the Other." A hunger not fed by the church's pharisaism it leads to solitude rather than community. His own role he perceives as having developed because "the tribe need a father who is afraid only / Of ceasing to love them well" (s. 20). He in turn must be fed by Jesus, but "Counting it better than bread to say the words of Christ," he prays for no easement, acknowledging suffering as "The only gate we have to paradise" (s. 22), and he is conscious of house and tribe, "Inhabited with the flame of non-possession. . . . Too simple a thing for the world to understand" (s. 23).

Sonnets 24 - 26 concern three members of the "tribe" — Barry, a mental patient and a "debutante," his arm tattooed: "Dad; Love; Hate"; Richard, "wary as a crayfish" and needing mother-love; and Rex, suffering physical torture but working on. These portraits lead to a sonnet on the MacDonald Crescent doss-house, with its three tribes — the drunks, the boobheads (drug addicts), and the students. A conclave of the drunks ("my own tribe") judges the town, to find, with a sense of the apocalyptic, that "it had already been judged."

From this point the sequence takes up the theme of tending the sick. Or, rather, that is an objective, observer's way of putting it. The protagonist must look after two of the women in the *wharepuni* who are sick. He finds it a nuisance to cook for them and would rather think about his poems, or go to Otaki and give talks to Catholic laymen, to "spout nonsense and wear my poverty/ As a coat of vanity." Prevented from following his desires by "The Joker who won't let me shuffle my own pack," he finds peace in being thwarted and recommends to his patients, for their whole health's sake, "Maoritanga," the Maori spirit of natural devotion. Then through a doctrinal argument with a priest he pursues this idea of playing one's alloted part, giving oneself entirely into God's hands:

> By his old habit,
> I'd say, God will let us wait till the boat is sinking
> Then bail us out in a minute.
>   (s. 35)

Then his thoughts flash back a whole decade to a leper lying beside the fruitstalls of Calcutta, who is used even by the flies like a carcass. Baxter had flung some coin into the beggar's tin dish, but a passing policeman said, "They're no use to him," obviously thinking it a useless gesture. At the utilitarian level at which we conduct our lives, this, of course, was true. "But the man was not quite dead," and the gesture was one of recognition that he was alive, that all living creatures need and deserve a loving hand and (most of all), however diminished and however demeaning the role they have to play, a sense of belonging to the tribe:

> Abe, with one lung
> Deflated, who would wheeze all night like a blowhole
>
> Behind a curtain in the top bunk,
> But I saw him with a shovel at the bottom of the pit
>
> They dug for the shithouse, tossing earth to the sky,
> His dark face wrinkled with the tribal smile.
>
> (s. 37)

Two sonnets follow on the subject of being marooned in the *wharepuni* in the rain; but through a dream the place is transformed into the ark (linking back with the conversation with the priest in sonnet 32: "There were eight souls, they say, with Father Noah; / Neither you nor I might have made it to the gangplank"). In sonnet 39 the ark-*wharepuni* becomes the tribal ark of survival:

> There has to be, I think, some shelter,
> A home, an all-but-God, an all-but-mother
>
> In time and place, not just the abstract void
> Of I looking for me.

Conversely (sonnet 40), the outside world, filled with inquisitive people beyond the tribe, seems threatening. God Himself offers no cure for the many kinds of death (sonnet 42), although nature has cures for natural ills (sonnet 43); but in this life "We make our darkness for ourselves," and God points to poverty as the way to peace (sonnet 44). As the sequence closes the writer plans to visit the outer world, "Where the sheep get more freedom than their masters" (sonnet 45). His ultimate message (and Baxter's late work is

The Way to the Upper Room

undeniably a message) is simple enough, namely, that "Fear is the only enemy" (sonnet 46). Fear of the natural self has, all along, been root cause of the puritanism Baxter fought.

The closing sonnet of this fine sequence (sonnet 48) is intensely interesting in relation to Baxter's whole career. It is a total acceptance of all the negative elements in himself and in life. The spider, tantric goddess, is Spiderwitch, the temptress, in profounder form — a manifestation of the Terrible Mother, or Great Mother. As Erich Neumann tells us:

> In so far as the Feminine releases what is contained in it to light and life, it is the Great and Good Mother of all life.
> On the other hand, the Great Mother in her function of fixation and not releasing what aspires toward independence and freedom is dangerous. This situation constellates essential phases in the history of consciousness and its conflict with the Archetypal Feminine. To this context belongs a symbol which plays an important role in myth and fairy tale, namely, captivity. This term indicates that the individual who is no longer in the original and natural situation of childlike containment experiences the attitude of the Feminine as restricting and hostile. Moreover, the function of ensnaring implies an aggressive tendency, which, like the symbolism of captivity, belongs to the witch character of the negative mother. Net and noose, spider, and the octopus with its ensnaring arms are here the appropriate symbols. The victims of this constellation have always acquired some element of independence, which is endangered; to them containment in the Great Mother is no longer a self-evident situation; rather, they have become "strugglers."[6]

Neumann says elsewhere that the spider is at the laybrinth's center, center of danger and center of discovery, a means of barring the way to wholeness and yet a means of ingress, hence the protagonist's closing prayer in *Autumn Testament*, "let me pass in peace." Neumann's spider is also "crab woman." In his concluding lines Baxter seems to merge this creature with the judging God, as "king crab / At the door of the underworld," but the daunting image is offset by the prayer and by the tone of acceptance which pervades the whole latter part of the poem.

Such an interpretation is backed up by a passage in the ensuing section, a prose "Letter to Colin" (Durning):

> At Hiruharama we go beyond the conscious shell of knowledge, that part of the soul which says — "I want; I have; I am" — into the darkness of

the anima, the yin principle in the mind which may be compared to the night itself. It is necessary to make this journey. The anima is the area familiar to Maori thought, the place of fear, the passive night from which dreams come, where one encounters the spirits of nature and the spirits of the dead. At times the journey may be agonising. It may demand the last ounce of oneself, to go beyond oneself, to walk the waters of availability to all things and all persons. But there is always peace beyond the agony. We wait to be turned into entire creatures. At the centre of the darkness we wait for the light of the spiritus to shine, the light that the disciples saw on the Mountain of Transfiguration.

(AT, 43)

Five remaining prose pages in this section consider various problems of the community (now no longer "open-door," but as a result of a series of social crises, including the closing of the commune, confined to ten *nga mokai*) and the individual soul, the struggle to attain and sustain belief, the need and inevitability of suffering, and the dream of Gehenna — the valley of ashes, which is our civilization of "guns and money and the badges of education" (AT, 48). Against it is the way of poverty, the road to man's true self.

A seven-part sonnet sequence, "Te Whiori O Te Kuri" (The Tail of the Dog) concludes *Autumn Testament*, a meditative summing-up of the detail and significance of life at the *wharepuni*, its strength in its note of particularized simplicity. Because, taken together, the Jerusalem writings constitute Baxter's greatest literary achievement, it is tempting to see them as climactic. But it is both to misunderstand and undervalue them if we consider them merely as pieces of literature and merely as a culmination. As Murray Edmond noted, the barriers of mode broke down — between prose and poem, between letter and diary, essay and sermon, between mere writing and life itself. Not so much an "adjunct" (Edmond's term), these writings are an integral part of a whole life, one which lived out its early aim, to be "a cell of good living in a corrupt society."

Finally, three other publications remain to be mentioned. Of these, the most recent, *The Labyrinth* (1974) is subtitled, *Some Uncollected Poems 1944 - 1972* and described by its editor as a "representative sampling" (of about one-seventh) from some four hundred uncollected poems. Intriguingly, much of the work in it, and from the whole period, is very fine, though detailed discussion would take us back yet again over the span of Baxter's entire career. The last twenty or more pages come from the latest work and include a more formal response to the Jerusalem period, "Five Sestinas."

The Way to the Upper Room   169

IX   Runes

Runes (1973), the final Oxford book, is something of a disappointment when placed alongside the Jerusalem work. The first third of the book consists of adaptations from Catullus, done with a degree of fluency and accomplishment, but not otherwise particularly remarkable. Worth noticing, perhaps, is that Baxter should choose at this unlikely stage of his life to adapt Catullus, that the section of poems is titled "Words to Lay a Strong Ghost," and that the recipient of many of them is apparently the Pyrrha of Baxter's Dunedin youth. Little, if anything remains of the joyful energy which is an essential part of the original, for these are poems, as one says, from "the edge of the impenetrable hymen/ Only the dead have broken." "Death is the one door out of the labyrinth!"

Section 2 of the book is dominated by a mood of reminiscence, its furniture very Baxterian: a Sunday stroll on the banks of the Leith stream, recollections of his daughter, in whose rebellion he perceives himself. As poems, the most fully realized are perhaps "Mother and Son" (despite one or two posturings) and "At Rakiura." A number of times through his career Baxter had used the image of the window, open to the night wind, or the door "ajar to let the Furies enter," inlets of fear and life. Here, in "The Millstones" (p. 48), seemingly addressed to his brother Terry, he concludes: "The gales of the south sea / Will hammer tonight on a shut window." "Letter from the Mountain," which closes the collection, ends:

Despair is the only gift;
When it is shared, it becomes a different thing; like rock, like water;
And so you also can share this emptiness with me.

Tears from faces of stone. They are our own tears.
Even if I had forgotten them
The mountain that has taken my being to itself
Would still hang over this hut, with the dead and the living
Twined in its crevasses. My door has forgotten how to shut.

X   *Vale*

In his brief valedictory paragraphs in *James K. Baxter 1926 -1972: A Memorial Volume* (1972), Denis Glover spoke of Baxter's "innate devious jesuitry," his humility which was "arrogant self-deception," and his personality, which Glover described (with a brand of humility of his own) as "much too tortuous for a simpleton like me."[7] This is the extreme counterstatement to the prevailing reverence and adulation of the first few months after Baxter's death. If nothing else, it points to Baxter as an enigma, to the undeniable excellence of his work (both personal and written) which derived from Jerusalem, to the puzzle (perhaps) presented by the Catullus translations, to a possible further puzzle (though maybe only to the literal-minded) suggested by a line in "Ode to Auckland": "Christianity has weakend my brain cells, brother."

The title poem of *Ode to Auckland and Other Poems* (1972), which has the special status of being the last poem Baxter wrote (dated 18 October 1972, a few days before his death) has something of the tone of a McDiarmid "Hymn to Lenin." It ends:

> How can I live in a country where the towns are made like coffins
> And the rich are eating the flesh of the poor
> Without even knowing it?
>
> O Father Lenin, help us in our great need!
> The people seem to enjoy building the pyramids.
> Moses would get a mighty cold reception.
> They'd kiss the arse of Pharaoh any day of the week
>
> For a pat on the head and a dollar note.
> At another time in another place
> Among the Ngati-Whatua
> When they brought the dead child into the meeting house
> She opened her eyes and smiled.

The exhortation to Lenin should tell us that Baxter's was no orthodox journey. What would have been his next direction? Perhaps he would have stopped writing altogether. We cannot tell, for he was a strangely complex man. What we do know is that when he died he was a public figure widely loved and respected for a constructive approach to human problems. As a poet, he is the most gifted so far produced by his country. Conscious perhaps of the near-presences of his Muse and Mary, the all-forgiving Mother, my mind has often come back during the writing of this book to the closing lines of "Pig Island Letters":

> As that wild nymph of water rises
> So does the God in man.

Notes and References

Chapter One

1. See Baxter's "Conversations with an Ancestor", MH, pp. 17 - 22.
2. *Penguin Book of New Zealand Verse*, ed. Allen Curnow (London, 1960), p. 313.
3. FA, p. 57. Hereafter cited in text.
4. Archibald Baxter, *We Will not Cease* (London, 1939; Christchurch, 1968).
5. PIL, p. 10. Book hereafter cited in text.
6. "Recollections of School Days," *Monthly Review*, March 1966, pp. 17 - 19.
7. *The Labyrinth*, p. 14.
8. "Essay on the Higher Learning," *The Spike* (Victoria University College, 1961), p. 62.
9. FH, p. 31, "A Rented Room." Book hereafter cited in text.
10. HB, p. 43, "Christchurch 1948." Book hereafter cited in text.
11. J. E. Weir, "The Green Inn: Some Reflections on the Poetry of James K. Baxter," *Comment*, April 1970, pp. 22 - 28.
12. *Recent Poetry in New Zealand*, ed. Charles Doyle (London and Auckland, 1965), p. 30.
13. Charles Doyle, *Small Prophets and Quick Returns* (Auckland, 1966), p. 11.
14. Notes taken by the present writer at a talk given at Auckland University in 1963.
15. James K. Baxter, *Aspects of Poetry in New Zealand* (Christchurch, 1967), p. 26.
16. J. E. Weir, *The Poetry of James K. Baxter* (Wellington, 1970), p. 14, quoting a letter Baxter to Weir 29 March 1961.
17. "The Yoke," in *New Zealand Poetry Yearbook*, ed. Louis Johnson (Christchurch, 1960), IX, 24.
18. Baxter, "Aspects of Indian Life," *Education*, no. 8 (June 1959), p. 78.
19. Ronald Barker, "NZ Play Draws Ecstatic Praise in South," *New Zealand Herald*, 19 December 1959.

20. Louis Johnson, "Writer Wise Choice for Burns Scholarship," *Dominion*, 23 October 1965. Baxter for some years in letters to his mother mentioned the idea that he should edit MacMillan Brown's memoirs. He provided one of three introductions to *The Memoirs of John MacMillan Brown* (Christchurch, 1974). The first and second were written by his mother and his aunt, the editing was done chiefly by his aunt.

21. Baxter to Maurice Shadbolt, 22 September 1963.

22. Barrie Watts, "Rebel Finds Peace in Sanctuary," *Sunday Times*, 14 June 1970, p. 15.

23. Ibid., p. 28.

24. Mervyn Dykes, "Commune Folk Seek Truth Down by the Riverside," *New Zealand Weekly News*, 4 January 1971, pp. 2 - 8.

25. *New Zealand Herald*, 8 April 1971.

26. *Sunday Times*, September 1971.

27. John Summers (Christchurch bookseller and poet) to present writer, 30 April 1973.

Chapter Two

1. *Trends*, p. 9. Hereafter cited in text.
2. *Beyond the Palisade*. Hereafter cited in text as BP.
3. W. Hart-Smith, "The Poetry of James K. Baxter," *Meanjin Papers* 11, no. 4 (1952), 386.
4. *A Book of New Zealand Verse*, ed. Allen Curnow (Christchurch, 1945), pp. 54 - 55.
5. Baxter, "On the Side of Life," *New Zealand Poetry Yearbook*, 4 (1954), 26.
6. Edward Thomas, *Collected Poems* (London, 1936), p. 94. Another New Zealand poet, Alistair Campbell, was in his early days much influenced by Thomas.
7. Weir, *The Poetry of James K. Baxter*, pp. 24 - 28.
8. Vincent O'Sullivan, "After Culloden: Remarks on the Early and Middle Poetry of James K. Baxter," *Islands* 2, no. 1 (Autumn 1973), 19 - 30.
9. Norman O. Brown, *Love's Body* (New York, 1966). See especially chapter 2.
10. Curnow, review of BWF, *Landfall* 2, no. 3 (September 1948), 233.
11. Baxter, Doyle, Johnson, Smithyman, *The Night Shift* (Wellington, 1957).
12. Erik Schwimmer, review of *The Night Shift*, *Numbers*, no. 9 (February 1959), pp. 63 - 64.
13. Baxter, "Cressida," *Landfall* 5, no. 2 (June 1951), 92 - 103.
14. *Poems Unpleasant*, hereafter cited in text as PU.

Notes and References

Chapter Three

1. This literary squabble continued from the early 1950s, after the second edition of Curnow's *A Book of New Zealand Verse*, up to the mid-1960s. Partially regionalist, partially a difference between generations, the quarrel also hinged on the issue of nationalism versus internationalism. Allen Curnow, spokesman for the generation of the 1930s, was also to a degree xenophobic when it came to direct outside influence on New Zealand life. Although his own work has been importantly influenced by overseas writers, particularly Yeats and Wallace Stevens, he deplored the intrusions of "overseas experts," and possible interference with the extremely delicate plant of indigenous New Zealand *pakeha* culture. Louis Johnson, a journalist (as Curnow had been), editor of the *New Zealand Poetry Yearbook* and *Numbers*, became the most persistent spokesman for internationalism and against "the New Zealand thing, the regional thing, the real thing" (a phrase of Curnow's, misappropriated). Curnow lived in Auckland, Johnson in Wellington. Johnson was supported by many of the group of Wellington poets, and a distinction grew up between Wellington "romanticism" and the work of Auckland poets, some consciously regionalist and others taking Curnow's view that there must be "a reality prior to the poem" (apparently of external nature). Headed by Johnson and Baxter, the Wellington poets tended to produce work which was a mixture of urban social commentary, psychomythology, and a sort of intuitive vaticism. Two Aucklanders, Kendrick Smithyman and Keith Sinclair, described themselves as "regionalists." In general, the work of the Auckland poets was (at least by intention) more rigorous, careful, and rational, but the whole scene there had less literary excitement than was available in Wellington.

The quarrel abated in the mid-1960s (partly because most of the "internationalist" poets had left for overseas, and some had begun to outgrow their youthful "romanticism"), but at the same time "public" interest in poetry diminished, to be revived by a new generation in the early 1970s. The quarrel itself may be traced in the pages of the *New Zealand Listener, Here and Now, Numbers,* and the *Poetry Yearbook*. One large element in it is the introduction to Curnow's *Penguin Book of New Zealand Verse*, a work in progress throughout the whole of the late 1950s, and the selection of the "younger poets" therein. One response to the Penguin anthology is *Recent Poetry in New Zealand* (1965); see also Kendrick Smithyman, *A Way of Saying* (Auckland, 1965).

2. Robert Chapman, review of FH, *Landfall* 7, no. 3 (1953), 210.

3. Robert Chapman and Jonathan Bennett, *An Anthology of New Zealand Verse* (London, 1956), Introduction. The internationalist attitudes expressed were anticipated by Baxter: "With the ordinary cultural background of an educated man, talent, and a mind alive to the meaning of

his experience, a New Zealand poet need be no more isolated than one living in London or Greenwich Village" (FA, 74).

4. *A Way of Saying*, p. 96; Smithyman points out that Baxter's attitude to childhood was not unequivocal (107 - 8). Chapman: "there are hints in later work of Mr. Baxter's that he sees his childhood less seraphically and not as a contrast to his adult life but as a cause of it." Nonetheless, the "myth" of the childhood garden remained important to Baxter throughout his life.

5. Allen Curnow, *A Small Room with Large Windows* (London, 1962), p. 41.

6. Ibid., p. 80.

7. "Prose Poems," *Salient Literary Issue*, July 1952, pp. 3 - 7.

8. Gaston Bachelard, *The Poetics of Space* (New York, 1964), translated by Maria Jolas, pp. 4, 6 - 7.

9. Rainer Maria Rilke, *The Notebooks of Malte Laurids Brigge* (New York, 1964), p. 26.

10. "Notes Towards an Aesthetic," *Salient Literary Issue*, July 1953, p. 28.

11. "Over the Tin Fence," *Numbers* 3, no. 3 (June 1955), 21 - 27.

12. "Notes Towards an Aesthetic," p. 30.

13. "Parable," *Numbers* 2, no. 2 (March 1957), 7 - 8.

14. Robert Chapman, review of FH, *Landfall* 7 (1953), 209 - 14.

15. Seddon and Savage were two prime ministers of New Zealand. Richard John Seddon (1845 - 1906) was premier 1893 - 1906 and introduced women's suffrage and old age pensions. Michael Joseph Savage (1872 - 1940) was first Labour premier of New Zealand (1935 - 1940) and was largely responsible for the country's large-scale adoption of social welfare policies, which he called "applied Christianity."

Chapter Four

1. Baxter, "Writing and Existence," *Education*, August 1963, pp. 16 - 19.

2. Thomas Crawford, review of HB, *Landfall* 16, no. 4 (December 1962), 394 - 96.

3. "Kilokery and Kalekhan," *Education*, February 1960, p. 21 - 24.

4. D. C. Walker, "Baxter's Notebook," *Landfall* 25, no. 1 (March 1971), 20 - 24.

5. *New Zealand Poetry Yearbook* 11 (1964), 12.

6. Baxter, "Notes," *Review*, '67, p. 4.

7. "Poetry and Education," pp. 3 - 4.

8. J. E. Weir, "Man without a mask: a study of the poetry of James K. Baxter" (M.A. Thesis, University of Canterbury, 1968), p. 66.

9. Walker, p. 20.

10. Baxter to Shadbolt, 22 September 1963.

11. Weir, "The Green Inn," p. 22.

Notes and References

Chapter Five

1. *Trends,* p. 16.
2. Charles Brasch, "Notes," *Landfall* 4, no. 3 (September 1950), 186 - 87.
3. FH, p. 35.
4. Bill Pearson, "Two Personal Memories of James K. Baxter: I," *Islands* 2, no. 1 (Autumn 1973), 3.
5. "Prose Poems," *Salient Literary Issue,* July 1952, p. 6.
6. Baxter papers, Hocken Library, University of Otago. Already cited in my Baxter article in *Ariel.*
7. *New Zealand Poetry Yearbook* 6 (1956 - 1957), 18 - 19.
8. Bill Pearson, "Fretful Sleepers," *Landfall* 6, no. 3, (September 1952), 201 - 30 (quoted from p. 224).
9. Weir, M. A. thesis, Appendix A; Baxter to Weir, 10 December 1962.
10. *New Zealand Poetry Yearbook* 4 (1954), 24.
11. "Letter to Eugene O'Sullivan," *The Labyrinth* (Wellington, 1974), p. 55.
12. *Six Faces of Love* (Wellington, 1972), unpaged (p. 46).

Chapter Six

1. *Recent Poetry in New Zealand,* p. 30.
2. *The Odyssey,* trans. Robert Fitzgerald (New York, 1963), p. 182.
3. Joseph Campbell, *The Hero with a Thousand Faces* (New York, 1956), p. 101.
4. *Salient Literary Issue,* July 1952, p. 34.
5. Baxter, *The Flowering Cross,* pp. 18 - 40. Book hereafter cited in text as FC.
6. Letter to present writer, October 1963.
7. "Kiwi Habits," *Review* '67 (University of Otago), pp. 8 - 9.
8. Baxter, *Ode to Auckland and Other Poems* (Dunedin, 1972), p. 13.
9. Baxter, *Poems* (Wellington, 1964), p. 22.
10. *Landfall,* September 1953, p. 212.
11. Baxter, *The Hero* (Dunedin, n.d.), 6p.

Chapter Seven

1. From Baxter's letter to *New Zealand Listener,* 29 October 1965.
2. FC, p. 16.
3. *New Zealand Listener,* 15 December 1967.
4. Review of IFN, *Landfall,* March 1959, p. 85.
5. O'Sullivan, *Islands* 2, no. 1 (Autumn 1973), 25.
6. *Tuatara* 8/9 (Fall 1972), 120.
7. Chapman, review of FH, p. 212.

Chapter Eight

1. Baxter, Introduction to *The Sore-Footed Man/The Temptations of Oedipus* (Auckland, 1971), pp. ix - x.
2. Baxter, Introduction to *The Devil and Mr. Mulcahy/The Band Rotunda* (Auckland, 1971), p. x.
3. Ibid., p. x.
4. Hal Smith, "Baxter's Theatre: A Critical Appraisal," in *James K. Baxter Festival: 1973: Four Plays* (Wellington, 1973), p. 3.
5. James Bertram, "The Wide Open Cage," *Landfall* 14, no. 4 (December 1960), 81 - 84.
6. "Jack Winter's Dream," *New Zealand Listener*, 19 September 1958, p. 8.
7. Baxter, *Two Plays: The Wide Open Cage and Jack Winter's Dream*, (Wellington, 1959), p. 37.
8. *Band Rotunda*, Introduction, p. vii.
9. O. E. Middleton, "Oedipus at Dunedin," *Landfall* 24, no. 2 (June 1970), 171 - 73.
10. Howard McNaughton, "Baxter as Dramatist," *Islands* 2, no. 2 (Winter 1973), 184 - 92.
11. *The Sore-Footed Man*, Introduction, p. vii.
12. Marilyn Parker, "Three Mimes," *Landfall* 22, no. 1 (March 1968), 63 - 65.

Chapter Nine

1. Tony Simpson, "Baxter at Jerusalem," *Cave*, no. 2 (August 1972), pp. 28 - 35.
2. Baxter, *Six Faces of Love* (Wellington, 1972), unpaged (pp. 41 - 42).
3. Murray Edmond, "The Idea of the Poet," *Cave*, no. 4 (November 1973), p. 36.
4. C. K. Stead, "Towards Jerusalem," *Islands* 2, no. 1 (Autumn 1973), 7 - 18.
5. Max Harris, Introduction to Baxter, *Two Obscene Poems* (Adelaide, 1973), unpaged.
6. Erich Neumann, *The Great Mother* (Princeton, N.J., 1972) p. 66.
7. *James K. Baxter 1926 - 1972: A Memorial Volume* (Wellington, 1972), p. 125.

Glossary of Maori Words

Ao-tea-Roa	New Zealand
aroha	love
haka	Maori war dance
kea	native NZ hawk
kiwi	wingless native bird, term used colloquially to refer to any New Zealand person
macrocarpa	native conifer, often shaped into windbreak
mana	prestige
manuka	native myrtle tree (also called ti tree)
Maoritanga	Maori tradition
marae	tribal meeting ground
nga mokai	the fatherless
paua	native shell fish, like abalone
Tangaroa	Maori sea-god
taniwha	water spirit
Te Whaea	the Source, the Mother of God
Tutanekai	Maori chief and legendary lover
Wahi Ngaro	the Void
wharepuni	meeting-house

(other terms are glossed in the text)

Appendix

Baxter's *Plays* (listed chronologically)

Jack Winter's Dream (1956)
The Wide Open Cage (1959)
The Silver Plate (1961)
Three Women and the Sea (1961)
The Spots on the Leopard (1962)
Mr Brandywine Chooses a Gravestone (1966)
The First Wife (1966)
The Bureaucrat (1967)
The Starlight in Your Eyes (1967)
The Band Rotunda (1967)
The Devil and Mr Mulcahy (1967)
Mr O'Dwyer's Dancing Party (1967)
The Sore-Footed Man (1967)
The Day Flanagan Died (1968)
The Temptations of Oedipus (1968)
Who Killed Sebastian (produced in 1969)

No date established:

The Runaway Wife
The Gentle Ones (Mr O'Dwyer's Dancing Party?)
To Catch a Hare
The Hero
The Rendezvous
The World Is (around 1961 - 1962?)

Baxter's three Mimes, *The Woman, The Axe and the Mirror,* and *The Cross* date from 1967

Selected Bibliography

PRIMARY SOURCES (listed chronologically)

1. Books and pamphlets (excluding broadsheets)

Beyond the Palisade (poems). Christchurch: The Caxton Press, 1944.
Blow, Wind of Fruitfulness (poems). Christchurch: The Caxton Press, 1948.
Recent Trends in New Zealand Poetry (criticism). Christchurch: The Caxton Press, 1951.
Poems Unpleasant (with Louis Johnson and Anton Vogt). Christchurch: The Pegasus Press, 1952.
The Fallen House (poems). Christchurch: The Caxton Press, 1953.
Traveller's Litany (a poem sequence). Wellington: The Handcraft Press, 1955.
The Fire and the Anvil (MacMillan Brown lectures, on modern poetry). Wellington: New Zealand University Press, 1955.
The Iron Breadboard (verse parodies). Wellington: The Mermaid Press, 1957.
The Night Shift (poems: with Charles Doyle, Louis Johnson, and Kendrick Smithyman). Wellington: Capricorn Press, 1957.
In Fires of No Return (poems selected and new). London: Oxford University Press, 1958.
Chosen Poems. Bombay: Konkan Institute of the Arts and Sciences, 1958 (printed for private circulation).
Two Plays: Jack Winter's Dream and The Wide Open Cage. Wellington: Capricorn Press, 1959.
Howrah Bridge and Other Poems (new and selected). London: Oxford University Press, 1961.
New Zealand in Colour (photographs by Kenneth and Jean Bigwood; text by Baxter). Wellington: Reed, 1961.
Poems (a magazine issue of selected poems). Wellington: Teachers' College, 1964.
Pig Island Letters (poems). London: Oxford University Press, 1966.

Aspects of Poetry in New Zealand (criticism). Christchurch: The Caxton Press, 1967.
The Lion Skin (poems). Dunedin: University of Otago Bibliography Room, 1967.
The Man on the Horse (lectures and articles in criticism, autobiography, and autobiographical fiction). Dunedin: University of Otago Press, 1967.
The Flowering Cross (articles on religion and conduct). Dunedin: The Tablet Press, 1967.
The Rock Woman: selected poems. London: Oxford University Press, 1969.
Jerusalem Sonnets. Dunedin: University of Otago Bibliography Room, 1970.
The Sore-Footed Man/The Temptations of Oedipus (plays). Auckland: Heinemann, 1971.
The Devil and Mr Mulcahy/The Band Rotunda (plays). Auckland: Heinemann, 1971.
Jerusalem Daybook (poems and prose). Wellington: Price Milburn, 1971.
Six Faces of Love (broadcast scripts on religion and conduct). Wellington: Futuna Press, 1972.
Letter to Peter Olds (poem sequence). Dunedin: Caveman Press, 1972.
Ode to Auckland and Other Poems. Dunedin: Caveman Press, 1972.
Autumn Testament (poems and prose). Wellington: Price Milburn, 1972.
The Tree House (poems for children). Wellington: Price Milburn, 1973.
Two Obscene Poems. Adelaide: privately printed, 1973.
The Labyrinth (some uncollected poems 1944 - 1972). Wellington: Oxford University Press, 1974.

2. Select List of Periodical Articles by Baxter (listed chronologically)

Review of John Mulgan's *Man Alone*. *Landfall* 3, no. 4 (December 1949, 374 - 76.
"Notes Towards an Aesthetic." *Salient Literary Issue*, September 1953.
"On the Side of Life." *New Zealand Poetry Yearbook* 3 (1954), 23 - 26.
"Dante in the Antipodes." *Numbers*, no. 2 (November 1954), pp. 1 - 2.
"Over the Tin Fence; A Consideration of the Life and Work of Oscar Wilde." *Numbers*, no. 3 (June 1955), pp. 21 - 27.
"The World of the Creative Artist." *Salient Literary Issue*, September 1955, pp. 20 - 26.
"Akitio: a country school and its community." *Education*, March 1958, pp. 41 - 48.
"Jack Winter's Dream: a discussion of the play and its music." *New Zealand Listener*, 19 September 1958, pp. 8 - 9.
"Aspects of Indian Life." *Education*, June 1959, pp. 77 - 79.
"Kilokery and Kalekhan: a study of Indian village life." *Education*, February 1960, pp. 21 - 24.
"Reply to a Questionnaire." *Landfall* 14, no. 1 (March 1960), 41 - 43.

Selected Bibliography

"Notes Made in Winter." *New Zealand Poetry Yearbook* 10 (1961 - 1962), 13 - 15.
"Writing and Existence." *Education*, August 1963, pp. 16 - 19.
"The Capital Graveyard." *Dominion*, 21 May 1970, pp. 11 - 12.

SECONDARY SOURCES

BAXTER, ARCHIBALD. *We Will Not Cease: The Autobiography of a Conscientious Objector* (London: Gollancz, 1939; Christchurch, Caxton Press, 1968)
BAYSTING, ARTHUR. Review of *Ode to Auckland*. *Landfall* 27, no. 4 (December 1973), 355 - 56.
BELL, BRIAN. "In the Fifties and Seventies." In *James K. Baxter 1926 - 1972: A Memorial Volume*, pp. 15 - 23. Wellington, 1972.
BENNETT, JONATHAN, and CHAPMAN, ROBERT. *An Anthology of New Zealand Verse*. London: Oxford University Press, 1956.
BERTRAM, JAMES. "The Wide Open Cage." *Landfall* 14, no. 4 (December 1960), 81 - 84.
―――. "A Poet of Extremes," in *James K. Baxter 1926 - 1972: A Memorial Volume*, 73 - 77.
CAMPBELL, ALISTAIR. "James K. Baxter: The Earlier Poems," *New Zealand's Heritage* (Sydney: Hamlyn House, 1971), 2561, 2564 - 2566.
―――. "Impressions of the Earlier Baxter," *Landfall*, vol. XXVII no. 3, September 1973, 179 - 84.
―――. "Hemi at Jerusalem," in *James K. Baxter 1926 - 1972: A Memorial Volume*, 55 - 57.
CHAPMAN, ROBERT. Review of *The Fallen House*, *Landfall*, vol. VII no. 3, Autumn 1953, 209 - 13.
―――, and BENNETT, JONATHAN, editors. *An Anthology of New Zealand Verse*. London: Oxford University Press, 1956.
CRAWFORD, THOMAS. Review of *Howrah Bridge and Other Poems*. *Landfall* 16, no. 4 (December 1962), 394 - 96.
CURNOW, ALLEN, ed. *A Book of New Zealand Verse*. Christchurch: Caxton Press, 1945; new edition 1951.
―――. Review of *Blow, Wind of Fruitfulness*. *Landfall* 2, no. 3 (September 1948), 233 - 35.
―――, ed. *Penguin Book of New Zealand Verse*. London, 1960.
DOYLE, CHARLES. "James K. Baxter: In Quest of the Just City." *Ariel* 5, no. 3 (July 1974), 81 - 98.
―――, ed. *Recent Poetry in New Zealand*. Auckland: Collins, 1965.
―――. *Small Prophets and Quick Returns*. Auckland: New Zealand Publishing Society, 1966.
EDMOND, MURRAY. "The Idea of the Poet." *Cave*, no. 4, pp. 29 - 39.
HARRIS, MAX. Introduction to Baxter's *Two Obscene Poems*. Adelaide: privately printed, 1973.

HART-SMITH, W. "The Poetry of James K. Baxter." *Meanjin Papers* II, no. 4 (1952), 382 - 90.

HIATT, BEN. Reviews of *Ode to Auckland* and *Runes*. *Second Coming* 1/2 (1974), 96 - 98, 100 - 101.

IRELAND, KEVIN. Review of *Pig Island Letters*. *Journal of Commonwealth Literature*, no. 4 (December 1967), pp. 139 - 40.

James K. Baxter 1926 - 1972: A Memorial Volume. Wellington: Alister Taylor, 1972.

LEEMING, OWEN. "And the Clay Man? Reflections on *The Rock Woman: Selected Poems* by James K. Baxter." *Landfall* 25, no. 1 (March 1971), 9 - 19. This gave rise to long letters of response by Baxter and J. E. Weir, published with Leeming's rejoinders in *Landfall* for June 1971, pp. 198 - 212 passim.

McCORMICK, E. H. *New Zealand Literature: A Survey*. London: Oxford University Press, 1959.

McKAY, F. M. *New Zealand Poetry: An Introduction*, Wellington: New Zealand University Press, 1970. pp. 61 - 68.

McNAUGHTON, HOWARD. "Baxter as Dramatist." *Islands* 2, no. 2 (Winter 1973), 184 - 92.

MIDDLETON, O. E. "Oedipus at Dunedin." *Landfall* 24, no. 2 (June 1970), 171 - 73.

MORITZ, ALBERT FRANK. Review of *Autumn Testament*. *Second Coming* 1/2 (1974), 102 - 7.

OLDS, PETER. "Two Personal Memories of James K. Baxter: II." *Islands* 2, no. 1 (Autumn 1973), 5 - 7. Olds also provided a brief introduction for Baxter's *Ode to Auckland and Other Poems*.

O'SULLIVAN, VINCENT. "After Culloden: Remarks on the Early and Middle Poetry of James K. Baxter." *Islands* 2, no. 1 (Autumn 1973), 19 - 30.

PARKER, MARILYN. "Three Mimes." *Landfall* 22, no. 1 (March 1968), 63 - 65.

PEARSON, BILL. "Two Personal Memories of James K. Baxter: I." *Islands* 2, no. 1 (Autumn 1973), 2 - 5.

REID, J. C., and WILKES, G. A. *The Literature of Australia and New Zealand*. Philadelphia: Pennsylvania State University Press, 1968.

RODDICK, ALAN. Review of *Aspects of New Zealand Poetry*. *Landfall* 21, no. 4 (December 1967), 388 - 89.

——. Review of *The Lion Skin*. *Landfall* 23, no. 1 (March 1969), 85 - 86.

SCHWIMMER, ERIK. Review of *The Night Shift*. *Numbers*, no. 9 (February 1959), pp. 63 - 64.

SIMPSON, TONY. "Baxter at Jerusalem." *Cave*, no. 2 (August 1972), pp. 28 - 35.

SMITH, HAL. "Baxter's Theatre: A Critical Appraisal." In *James K. Baxter Festival: 1973: Four Plays*, pp. 3 - 5, 12 - 13, 16. Wellington: Victoria University, 1973.

Selected Bibliography

SMITH, HAROLD W. "James K. Baxter: The Poet as Playwright." *Landfall* 22, no. 1 (March 1968), 56 - 62.
SMITHYMAN, KENDRICK. *A Way of Saying.* Auckland: Collins, 1965.
STEAD, C. K. Review of *In Fires of No Return* and *The Iron Breadboard. Landfall* 13, no. 1 (March 1959), 85 - 90.
———. "Towards Jerusalem: The Later Poetry of James K. Baxter." *Islands* 2, no. 1 (Autumn 1973), 7 - 18.
STEVENS, JOAN. "Mr. Baxter's Progress," review of *Howrah Bridge and Other Poems. New Zealand Listener,* 18 May 1962.
WALKER, D. C. "Baxter's Notebook," on *Jerusalem Sonnets. Landfall* 25, no. 1 (March 1971), 20 - 24.
WEIR, J. E. "Man Without a Mask: A Study of the Poetry of James K. Baxter." M.A. thesis, University of Canterbury, 1968.
———. *The Poetry of James K. Baxter.* Wellington: Oxford University Press, 1970.
———. "The Green Inn: Some Reflections on the Poetry of James K. Baxter." *Comment,* April 1970, pp. 22 - 28.
WINANS, A. D. "James K. Baxter (1926 - 1972)." *Second Coming* 1/2 (1974), 6 - 10.

Index

Adcock, Fleur, 15
Arachne, 64
Aristotle, 134 - 37, 139
Auden, W. H., 25, 38, 74

Baxter, Archibald, 14, 20 - 21, 93, 94, 135
Baxter, Jacquie (see under Sturm, J. C.)
Baxter, James K.: birth, 20; early schooling, 21 - 22; childhood visit to Europe, 22 - 24; early literary influences, 25 - 28; friendship with Louis Johnson, 29 - 30, 64 - 66, 72; trip to Asia, 31 - 31; Burns Fellowship, 32 - 33; at Jerusalem, 33 - 36, 52, 99, 155 - 68; and Maoris, 33 - 35, 41, 89 - 90, 155 - 68

WORKS: PLAYS
"Axe and the Mirror, The", 141, 142
Band Rotunda, The, 16, 33, 110, 136, 142, 144, 146 - 47
"Bureaucrat, The", 16, 33, 140, 142
"Cross, The", 141, 142
"Day Flanagan Died, The", 179
Devil and Mr Mulcahy, The, 16, 33, 133, 136, 140, 141, 145, 147 - 48
"First Wife, The", 138
Hero, The, 116 - 117, 139
Jack Winter's Dream, 62, 135, 136, 138, 140
"Jack Winter's Dream", 15, 34
"Mr. Brandywine Chooses a Gravestone", 139, 145
Mr. O'Dwyer's Dancing Party, 140, 145
"Rendezvous, The", 141

"Runaway Wife, The", 142
"Silver Plate, The", 141
Sore-Footed Man, The, 16, 33, 105, 140, 141, 143, 145 - 147
Spots on the Leopard, The, 16, 33, 139
"Starlight in Your Eyes, The", 141
Temptations of Oedipus, The, 16, 33, 137, 140 - 41, 142, 143 - 44, 145 - 46, 159
"Three Women and the Sea", 179
"Who Killed Sebastian?", 179
Wide Open Cage, The, 16, 32, 135, 139, 143, 145, 146
"Woman, The", 141, 142
"World Is, The", 141

WORKS: POETRY
"Advantages of Not Being Educated, The", 73
"Antelopes, The", 44,
"Apple Tree, The", 75, 132
"At Akitio", 71
"At Aramoana", 92
"At Rakiura", 169
"At Rotorua", 154
"At Taieri Mouth", 123
"Auckland", 71
Autumn Testament, 36, 132, 163 - 68
"Autumn Testament", 164 - 67
"Autumn Waking", 56
"Ballad of Calvary Street", 75, 94 - 95, 96, 131, 151
"Ballad of One Tree Hill", 84
"Baron Saturday", 108, 115
"Bay, The", 45 - 46, 71, 87
"Beach House, The", 121

185

Beyond the Palisade, 14, 25, 38 - 41, 87, 89, 90, 107, 115, 124, 132, 153
Blow, Wind of Fruitfulness, 14, 28, 41 - 51, 87, 90, 100, 119, 124, 149, 153
"Bucket of Blood for a Dollar, A", 98
"Canticle of the Desert", 112
"Cave, The", 47 - 50
Chosen Poems, 15
"Christchurch 1948", 26
"Christmas Poem", 44
"Clown's Coat, The", 70
"Cold Hub, The", 121
"Conversation in a Road", 52
"Cressida", 51 - 52, 76, 129
"Crossing Cook Strait", 70 - 71
"Dark Side, The", 54
"death song for mr mouldybroke, a", 98
"Divorcée", 108, 128
"Doll, The", 57, 59 - 60, 111
"Eagle", 38
"East Coast Journey", 83, 154
"Eioko", 128
"Elegy at the Year's End", 62, 66, 70, 71, 95 - 96
"Elegy for an Unknown Soldier", 101
"Elegy for My Father's Father", 46
Fallen House, The, 15, 41, 55 - 62, 87, 106
"Fallen House, The", 61 - 62
"Family Photograph 1939, A", 24
"Farmhand", 50, 101
"Fire in the Mountains", 39
"First Communions, The", 84, 126
"First Forgotten, The", 115
"Fishermen", 123
"Fitz Drives Home the Spigot", 109
"For Kevin Ireland", 108
"For My Father", 57
"For One Going Overseas", 44
"Girl in Yellow Jeans, The", 127
"Glass Door, The", 44
"Green Beret, The", 98
"Haast Pass", 47, 119, 132
"Harlot, The", 122, 128
"Henley Pub", 54, 84, 107, 108, 118, 123 - 24, 125, 127, 128, 129
"High Country Weather", 45
"Hollow Place, The", 83

"Homecoming, The", 53 - 54, 101
Howrah Bridge and Other Poems, 16, 32, 66, 73 - 76, 104, 106, 108, 109 - 110, 125, 128, 132, 133, 151
"Husband", 128
"Inflammable Woman, The", 108
In Fires of No Return, 15, 66 - 71, 73, 95 - 96, 104, 115, 127, 133, 151
Jerusalem Daybook, 17, 36, 59, 96, 158 - 62
Jerusalem Sonnets, 16, 35, 155 - 58
"Joke, The", 72
"Jottings", 131
"Journey, The", 102 - 103
"Killing of a Rabbit, The", 38
Labyrinth, The, 17, 96 - 97, 162, 168
"Lament for Barney Flanagan", 66, 68 - 70, 78
"Lazarus", 113, 150
"Letter to Noel Ginn, I", 119
"Letter to Noel Ginn, II", 46, 107
Letter to Peter Olds, 17, 36, 162 - 63
"Letter to the World", 127
"Let Time Be Still", 46, 132
"Lie Deep, My Love", 121
Lion Skin, The, 16, 33, 87, 108 - 109, 128
"Love Lyric, II", 37 - 38
"Love Lyric, IV", 39, 40
"Mill Girl", 52, 53, 96
"Millstones, The", 169
"Morning and Evening Calm", 49
"Mother and Son", 169
"Mountains, The", 38 - 39, 124
"My Love Late Walking", 132
"Near Kapiti", 83
"Never No More", 52
Night Shift, The, 14, 15, 30, 51 - 52, 87, 133
"Not-Yet-Made, The", 116
"Ode to Auckland", 170
Ode to Auckland and Other Poems, 17, 36, 170
"Old Earth Closet, The", 111
"Old Photograph, An", 72 - 73
"On the Death of Her Body", 75, 132
"O Wind Blowing", 49 - 50
"Paper Mask, The", 72
"Perfect Wife, The", 108

Index

"Perseus", 106
Pig Island Letters, 16, 21, 24 - 25, 33, 71, 75, 76 - 87, 88, 94, 111, 114, 115, 116, 118, 120, 121, 126, 127, 131, 133, 151 - 52, 153, 170
"Pig Island Letters", 21, 24 - 25, 76 - 82, 94, 114, 120, 126, 131, 170
"Poem Against Comfort", 113
"Poem By the Clock Tower, Sumner", 61, 150
"Poem in the Matukituki Valley", 60
Poems, 16
Poems Unpleasant, 15, 30, 52 - 54, 124, 127
"Postman", 82 - 83
"Private Conference of Harry Fat, The", 93 - 94
"Prometheus", 42 - 43
"Prose Poems", 92
"Prospector", 57, 58 - 59, 111
"Question of Rape, A", 108
"Rented Room, A", 57, 58
"Return, The", 104
"Returned Soldier", 44 - 45
"Revenants", 150
"Rocket Show", 71, 132
Rock Woman, The, 33, 87, 123, 126, 127 - 28, 153,
"Rope for Harry Fat, A", 74, 75, 93, 112
"Rotorua", 121
Runes, 169
"School Days", 22 - 23
"Sea Noon", 42
"Seraphion", 62, 66, 67
"Seven-Year-Old Poet", 84
"She Who is Like the Moon", 75, 132
"Sisyphus", 72
"Sixties, The", 30
"Small Ode on Mixing Flatting, A", 131
"Song", 72
"Song for an Old Soak", 57, 58
"Songs of the Desert", 51
"Surfman's Story, The", 52, 53, 127
"Takapuna Businessman Considers His Son's Death in Korea, A", 82, 96

"Temple Basin", 57
"Tempter, The", 104
"Thoughts of a Remuera Housewife", 82, 128
"Thrushes", 60, 150
"To a Print of Queen Victoria", 82
"To a Travelling Friend", 113
"To God the Son", 70, 151
"Tomcat", 82, 111, 122
"To My Father", 132
"To My Wife", 150
"Track, The", 46, 119, 132
Traveller's Litany, 15, 62 - 62, 76, 87, 123, 126
Tree House, The, 17, 154
"Tunnel Beach", 46, 47, 119 - 120, 132
Two Obscene Poems, 17, 163
"Venetian Blinds", 57 - 58
"Virginia Lake", 57
"Wapatiki Beach", 83, 124, 153 - 54
"Waves, The", 80
"What Shall We Seek For", 120
"Wild Bees", 61, 87
"Yoke, The", 31

WORKS: PROSE
Aspects of New Zealand Poetry, 16, 33
"Dante in the Antipodes", 150 - 51
Fire and the Anvil, The, 15, 24, 57, 62, 84, 89, 90, 91, 96, 107, 110, 111, 151
Flowering Cross, The, 16, 33, 109, 122 - 23, 125, 130, 133, 152 - 54
"Kilokery and Kalekhan", 74
Man on the Horse, The, 16, 21, 24, 25, 27 - 28, 31, 33, 40, 49, 54, 78, 84 - 86, 88, 89, 91, 92, 97, 98, 99, 104, 105, 107, 111, 112 - 13, 114, 115, 120, 123 - 24, 125, 127, 129, 149, 151, 153
New Zealand in Colour, 32
"Notes Towards an Aesthetic", 63, 66, 105
"Over the Tin Fence", 66 - 68
"Poetry and Education", 93
Recent Trends in New Zealand Poetry, 15, 41, 61, 64, 88, 90, 93, 97, 115, 149, 161
Six Faces of Love, 17, 99, 154 - 55
"Writing and Existence", 72

Baxter, Mrs Millicent (nee MacMillan Brown), 20
Baxter, Richard, 79 - 80
Baxter, Terry, 21, 169
Beckett, Samuel, 141 - 42
Bell, Brian, 15, 56
Bertram, James, Prof., 135, 137
Blake, William, 21
Bland, Peter, 16, 65
Brasch, Charles, 14, 26, 64, 90 - 91
Brecht, Bertolt, 141
Brown, Norman O., 101, 102
Burns, Robert, 21, 38, 85 - 86, 113 - 14, 124
Burton, Ormond, 14
Byron, Lord, 21

Campbell, Alistair, 15, 28, 52, 55, 64
Campion, Richard, 135
Carey, Patric, 35, 134
Catullus, 169, 170
Chapman, Robert, Prof., 55 - 56, 68, 132 - 33, 150
Chekhov, Anton, (*Three Sisters*), 138
Crane, Hart, 106
Crawford, Thomas, 73 - 74, 75
Curnow, Allen, 14, 15, 26 - 27, 41, 42, 50, 55, 56, 64, 98, 99, 124, 149, 173n1; *A Book of New Zealand Verse*, 14, 26

Darkness at Noon (Koestler), 92
De Profundis (Wilde), 67
Doyle, Charles, 15, 29, 32, 51, 64, 65
Duggan, Maurice, 65
Durning, Colin, 115, 167 - 68
Durrell, Lawrence, 32, 74, 76

Earth Meditations (Doyle), 65
Edmond, Murray, 155, 168
Eliot, T. S., 46, 124
Ellul, Jacques, 141
Empson, William, 38

Fairburn, A. R. D., 14, 25, 50, 78, 80
"Fretful Sleepers", (Pearson), 95
Freud, Sigmund, 30, 48

Giraudoux, Jean, 142 - 43
Glover, Denis, 15, 26, 27, 64, 75, 92, 111 - 12, 169
Greene, Graham, 92, 95, 144

Hardy, Thomas, 74
Harris, Max, 17, 163
Hero With a Thousand Faces, The, (Campbell), 103 - 104
Hesse, Hermann, 91
Hilliard, Noel, 52, 64
Hilltop, 64
Holcroft, M. H., 50, 63, 65, 99
Hood, Thomas, 21
Hope, A. D., 16
Hopkins, G. M., 38
Hughes, George, Rev. Prof., 15, 31
Hugo, Victor, 38
Humphries, Barry, 138

Johnson, Louis, 15, 29 - 30, 32, 33, 34, 51, 55, 63, 64, 65, 72, 92, 115, 173n1
Jung, C. G., 25, 30, 40, 68, 111

Kitto, H. D. F., 135

Landfall, 14, 16, 26, 65, 77, 84
Lawrence, D. H., 149
Lawson, Henry, 21, 25
Leeming, Owen, 62, 77
Lessing, Doris, 127
Lilburn, Douglas, 14
London Magazine, 16
Lorca, Federico Garcia, 140
Lowell, Robert, 76, 77, 89
Lowry, R. W., 16, 71, 92, 115

MacMillan Brown, John, Prof., 20, 21, 32
MacNeice, Louis, 25, 39, 74
Mannin, Ethel, 25
Marsh, Ngaio, 142
Mason, R. A. K., 41, 50
May, Rollo, 100
McCahon, Colin, 15, 92, 115
McNaughton, Howard, 137, 138, 139, 142, 144
Middleton, O. E., 137
Mitcalfe, Barry, 52, 64, 98

Neill, A. S., 25
Neumann, Erich, 167
New Zealand Listener, The, 15, 63, 84, 136, 137
Notebooks of Malte Laurids Brigge, The, (Rilke), 62
Numbers, 15, 16, 30, 63 - 66

Index

Oedipus at Colonnus (Sophocles), 145
Oliver, W. H., 64
O'Neill, Eugene, 139, 140
O'Sullivan, Eugene, Rev., 115
O'Sullivan, Vincent, 48 - 49, 126, 128

Parker, Marilyn, 142
Pearson, Bill, 92, 95
Penguin New Writing, 25
People's Voice, The, 63
Poetics of Space, The, (Bachelard), 58
Poetry Yearbook, 15, 16, 29, 41, 55, 63, 64, 72, 73, 102, 103, 112, 120, 122, 123, 127, 130

Recent Poetry in New Zealand, (Doyle), 16, 79, 100
Rilke, Rainer Maria, 58, 62
Rimbaud, Arthur, 16, 38, 84, 126

Sargeson, Frank, 95
Sartre, Jean-Paul, 142
Savage, Michael Joseph, Rt. Hon., 94
Schwimmer, Erik, 16, 51, 64, 65
Seddon, Richard John, Rt. Hon., 94
Shadbolt, Maurice, 21, 33, 76 - 77, 78 - 79, 80, 115
Shelley, P. B., 21
Simpson, Tony, 154, 155
Smith, Hal, 134, 140

Smithyman, Kendrick, 15, 51, 55, 56, 77
Snyder, Gary, 41, 115
Stead, C. K., 77, 124, 158
Strindberg, August, 135, 137, 140
Sturm, J. C. (Mrs. Jacquie Baxter), 26, 28, 65, 163 - 64
Summers, John, 36
Sun Among the Ruins, The, (Johnson), 29
Synge, J. M., 135, 140

Tamplin, Ronald, 16
Thomas, Dylan, 38, 64, 74, 135 (Under Milk Wood), 140
Tolstoi, L. N., 38, 139, 154
Tuwhare, Hone, 98

Valéry, Paul, 49
Vogt, Anton, 15, 52, 56, 64

Walker, D. C., 74, 77
Watts, Barrie, 34
Way of Saying, A (Smithyman), 56
Weir, J. E., 26, 31, 46, 49, 71, 74, 77, 80, 87, 95, 115, 133, 150, 153 - 54
We Will Not Cease (Archibald Baxter), 14
Wilde, Oscar, 66 - 68
Witheford, Hubert, 64

Yeats, W. B., 26, 38, 74

PR
9639
.3
.B3
Z63

256 -a

Doyle, Charles
James K. Baxter

The Library
Lynchburg College
Lynchburg, Virginia 24504

DEC 76